Descriptive Geometry Worksheets

Worksheets

with Computer Graphics

Series B

9th Edition

E. G. Paré
Lecturer at Loyola Marymount College

R. O. Loving
*Professor Emeritus of Engineering Graphics
and Formerly Chairman of the Department
Illinois Institute of Technology*

I. L. Hill
*Professor Emeritus of Engineering Graphics
and Formerly Chairman of the Department
Illinois Institute of Technology*

R. C. Paré
*Associate Professor of Mechanical Engineering Technology
University of Houston, Houston, Texas*

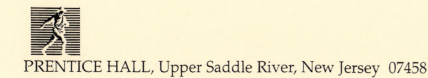
PRENTICE HALL, Upper Saddle River, New Jersey 07458

Acquisitions editor: *Eric Svendsen*
Production editor: *Barbara Kraemer*
Production supervisor: *Barbara Murray*
Production Coordinator: *Julia Meehan*

©1997 by Prentice-Hall, Inc.
Simon & Schuster/A Viacom Company
Upper Saddle River, New Jersey 07458

Printed in the United States of America

10 9 8 7 6 5 4 3 2 1

ISBN 0-02-391344-4

Prentice-Hall International (UK) Limited, *London*
Prentice-Hall of Australia Pty. Limited, *Sydney*
Prentice-Hall Canada Inc., *Toronto*
Prentice-Hall Hispanoamericana, S.A., *Mexico*
Prentice-Hall of India Private Limited, *New Delhi*
Prentice-Hall of Japan, Inc., *Tokyo*
Simon & Schuster Asia Pte. Ltd., *Singapore*
Editora Prentice-Hall do Brasil, Ltda., *Rio de Janeiro*

Symbols for Use on Drawings

TL — **True Length**
EV — **Edge View**
TS — **True Size**
LI — **Line of Intersection**

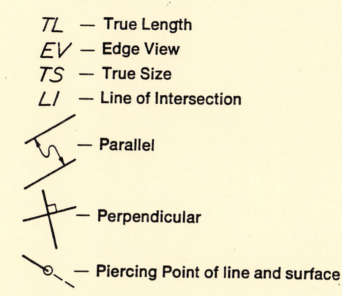

— **Parallel**

— **Perpendicular**

— **Piercing Point of line and surface**

Symbols for Instructor's Corrections

C — **Show construction**
D — **Show dimensions; show given or required data**
I — **Improve form or spacing**
H — **Too heavy**
NH — **Not heavy enough**
ND — **Not dark enough**
SL — **Sharpen pencil or compass lead**
GL — **Use guide lines**
A — **Improve arrowheads**

— **Error in encircled area**

Equivalents

inches to millimeters		millimeters to inches	
in.	mm	mm	in.
0.001	0.025	1	0.039
0.002	0.051	2	0.079
0.003	0.076	3	0.118
0.004	0.102	4	0.158
0.005	0.127	5	0.197
0.006	0.152	6	0.236
0.007	0.178	7	0.276
0.008	0.203	8	0.315
0.009	0.229	10	0.394
0.010	0.254	12	0.472
0.020	0.508	16	0.630
0.030	0.762	20	0.787
0.040	1.016	25	0.984
0.050	1.270	30	1.181
0.060	1.524	35	1.378
0.070	1.778	40	1.575
0.080	2.032	45	1.772
0.090	2.286	50	1.968
0.100	2.540	55	2.165
0.200	5.080	60	2.362
0.300	7.620	65	2.559
0.400	10.160	70	2.756
0.500	12.700	75	2.953
0.600	15.240	80	3.150
0.700	17.780	85	3.346
0.800	20.320	90	3.543
0.900	22.860	95	3.740
1.000	25.400	100	3.937

LENGTH	1 millimeter (mm) = .0393701 inch (in.) 1 inch (in.) = 25.4 millimeter (mm)
AREA	1 square millimeter (mm²) = 0.00155 square inch (in.²) 1 square inch (in.²) = 645.16 square millimeter (mm²)
MASS	1 kilogram (kg) = 2.20462 pound (lb) 1 pound (lb) = 0.453592 kilogram (kg)
FORCE	1 Newton (N) = 9.80665 kg·m/s²

Preface

Descriptive Geometry Worksheets, Series B is intended primarily for use with Descriptive Geometry, 9th Edition by the same authors and also published by Prentice-Hall. The group number identifications of the individual worksheets parallel the chapters of that textbook. However, this workbook may be used with any good descriptive geometry or comprehensive engineering graphics text.

Time available for teaching is limited. The objective of this workbook is to eliminate repetitious drawing and setup and allow the student to spend time learning theory and application. It is intended that the problems be solved by the widely accepted "direct" method. The layouts are designed so that either "folding line" or "reference plane" notation may be used. Good drafting practices should be followed to produce acceptable accuracy. All construction lines should be made lightly and should not be erased.

This workbook of descriptive geometry problems has been prepared by the authors, as an answer to the question frequently posed by students: "What use will I make of descriptive geometry?" Many practical applications presented in the problems speak for themselves. With but a few exceptions each worksheet contains at least one interesting practical application, many of which were suggested by a variety of industrial concerns.

Practical problems have not been used merely because they are practical, however. They are used only where the authors consider that they teach the theory involved at least as well as the corresponding abstract exercise. In general, each new division of subject matter is introduced with theoretical problems to focus the student's attention on the fundamentals involved. These are usually followed by applications to practical situations to make obvious the utility of the subject matter.

The use of many pictorial illustrations and the problems in pictorial form serve to stimulate interest and to contribute toward the development of three-dimensional visualization.

As in the case with the new 9th edition of the textbook, additional worksheets have been included in Group 14 to reflect new material in vectors, beams and trusses.

A number of problems are given in Group 24 to provide the student with essential training in problem layout. These problems also serve as comprehensive review material, since their solutions require the use of a number of the fundamentals.

A selected sample of computer graphics projects has been provided in Group 25. The computer graphics solutions demonstrate how mathematics and the computer can be combined to provide solutions to problems solved manually in the earlier groups.

To conform to the latest trends, all measurements are given with metric values. A conversion table and some metric scales are included for the student's convenience.

Since Series A of the Descriptive Geometry Worksheets also follows the same organization pattern, either workbook may be used with only minor schedule changes.

E.G.P.
R.O.L.
I.L.H.
R.C.P.

Contents

Text references may be found in Paré, Loving, Hill, and Paré, *Descriptive Geometry*, Ninth Edition (Prentice Hall, 1997). For convenient reference, the chapter numbers and titles in the text correspond to the group numbers and titles herein.

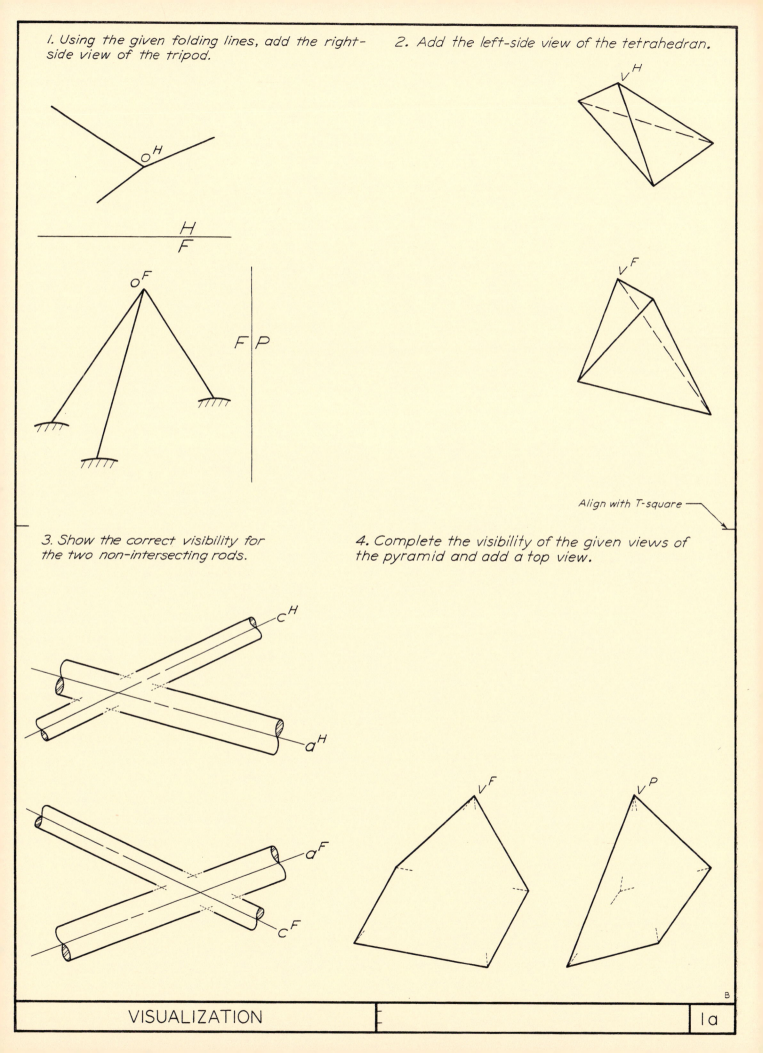

1. Using the given folding lines, add the right-side view of the tripod.

o^H

$\dfrac{H}{F}$

o^F

$F \mid P$

2. Add the left-side view of the tetrahedran.

V^H

V^F

Align with T-square

3. Show the correct visibility for the two non-intersecting rods.

c^H

a^H

a^F

c^F

4. Complete the visibility of the given views of the pyramid and add a top view.

V^F

V^P

VISUALIZATION

1a

B

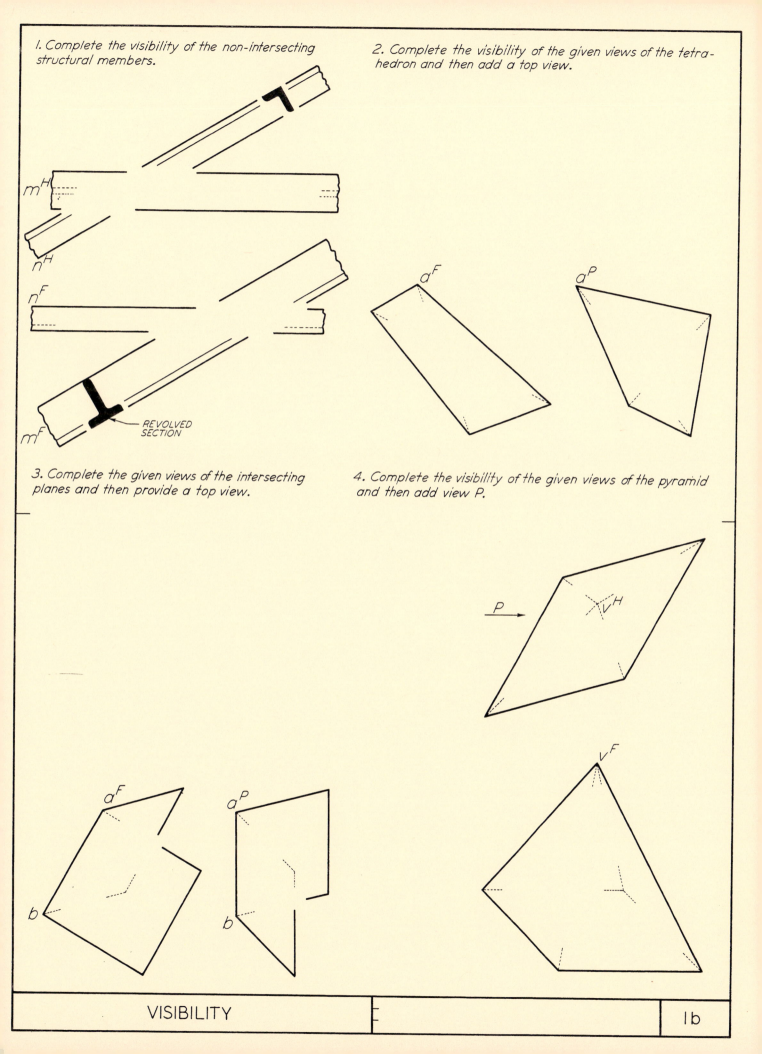

1. Complete the visibility of the non-intersecting structural members.

m^H

n^H

n^F

m^F

REVOLVED SECTION

2. Complete the visibility of the given views of the tetra-hedron and then add a top view.

a^F

a^P

3. Complete the given views of the intersecting planes and then provide a top view.

a^F

a^P

b

b

4. Complete the visibility of the given views of the pyramid and then add view P.

P

v^H

v^F

VISIBILITY

1b

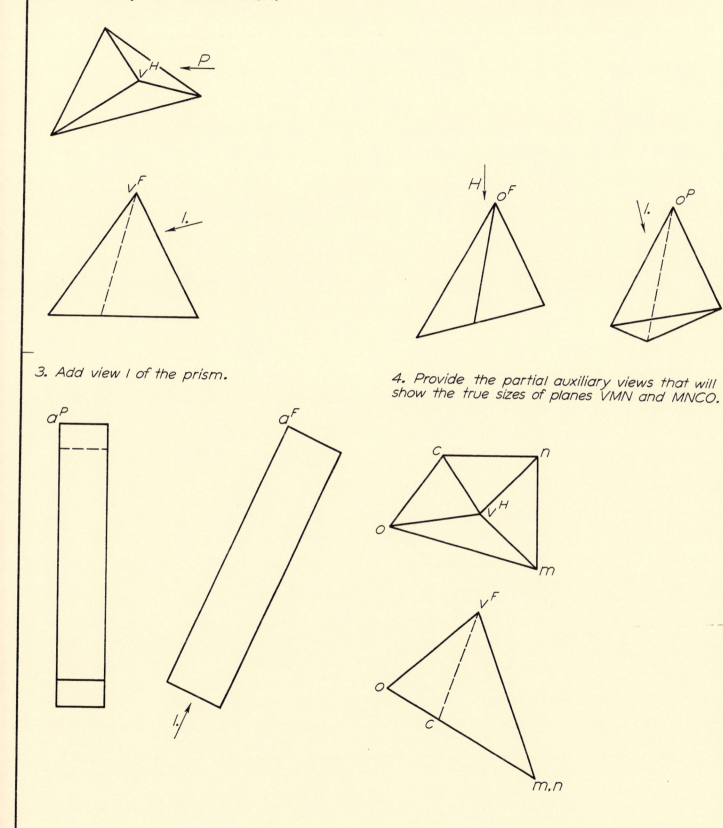

1. Draw the side view and auxiliary views of the pyramid as indicated by the arrows P and I.

2. Add the views H and I.

3. Add view I of the prism.

4. Provide the partial auxiliary views that will show the true sizes of planes VMN and MNCO.

PRIMARY AUXILIARY VIEWS

2a

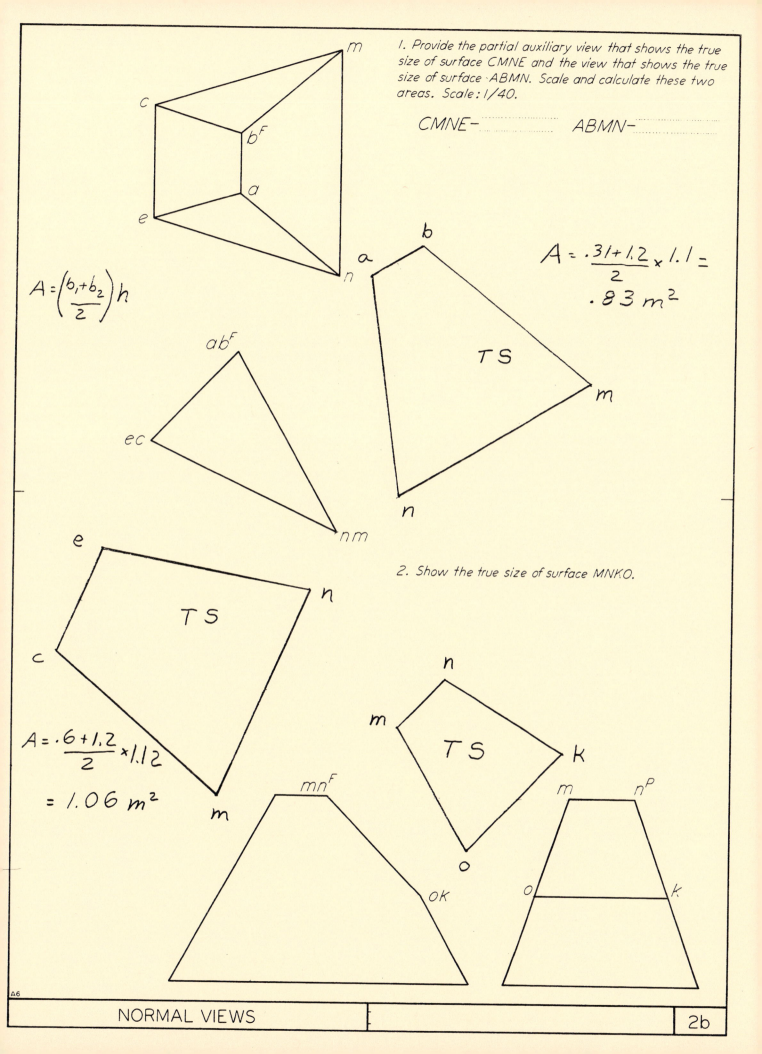

1. Provide the partial auxiliary view that shows the true size of surface CMNE and the view that shows the true size of surface ABMN. Scale and calculate these two areas. Scale: 1/40.

CMNE— ....   ABMN— ....

$A = \left(\dfrac{b_1 + b_2}{2}\right)h$

$A = \dfrac{.31 + 1.2}{2} \times 1.1 =$

$.83\ m^2$

ab^F

ec

nm

TS

$A = \dfrac{.6 + 1.2}{2} \times 1.12$

$= 1.06\ m^2$

TS

2. Show the true size of surface MNKO.

TS

mn^F

ok

n^P

A6

1. Find and label the true length (TL) of each tripod leg.

2. Find and label the TL of the edges AE, AB, VA and VB.

3. Obtain θ_H for line NK, θ_F for line VN, and θ_H for line VK.

$NK - \theta_H =$ ....
$VN - \theta_F =$ ....
$VK - \theta_H =$ ....

3.

θ_{VK}

4. For line AB, $\theta_P = 35°$. Complete the front view.

4.

a^P $+a^F$

5.

θ_H

5. Line VW has a downward slope of 20°.
Complete the front view of line VW.

A6

TRUE LENGTHS & ANGLES   3a

1. Detemine the length and grade of cableway AB. Scale: 1/400 000.

2. A 400 m pipeline MN bears N130° on a down-grade of 40%. Complete the given views. Scale: 1/500 000.

a^H

m^{H+}

b

a^F

b

$\underset{+}{m^F}$

H

F

AB:

Length = ...

Grade = ...

3. Determine the angles formed by the support frame and the surfaces to which they are attached.

Angles:

θ.... = ...

θ... = ...

o^H

o^F

BEARING, GRADE, & ANGLES

3b

1. Complete the front view of intersecting lines AB and CE.

2. Complete the top view of intersecting lines MN and OK. Establish the bearing, grade, and the TL of OK. Scale = 1:500

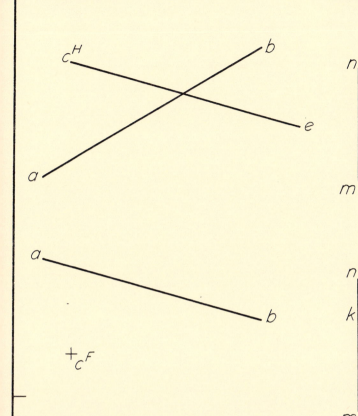

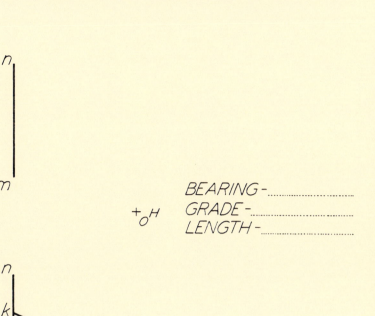

BEARING - ....
GRADE - ....
LENGTH - ....

3. The antenna of a transmitter is at location T and the base of a receiver is at location R. Obtain the minimum height (h) that must be exceeded by the receiver to provide a line-of-sight that clears the obstruction. Scale = 1:400

4. For the isometric pictorial, provide a line KS in plane P that intersects line AB. Add a line CE in plane H that intersects line AB.

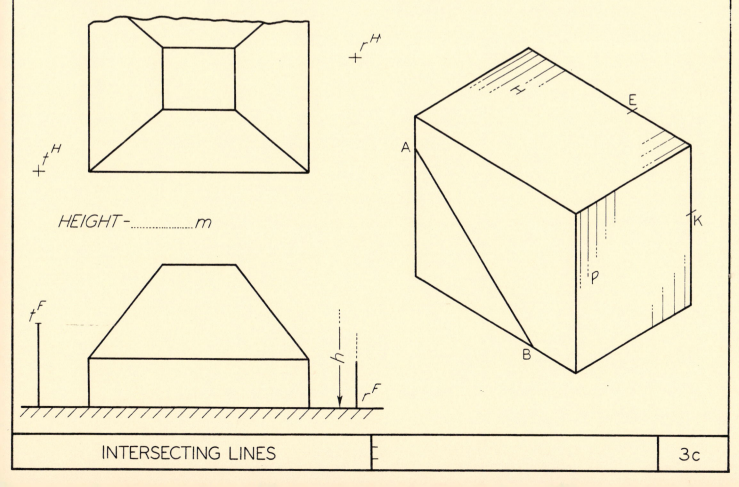

HEIGHT - .... m

1. Locate the top view of point B that lies in plane MNO. Locate the front view of point C that lies in this same plane.

n^H

m

o

$+c^H$

o

$+b^F$

m

n^F

2. In the given plane, add a frontal line through point A and add a horizontal line through point B. Label the TL of these principal lines.

a^H

b

a^F

b

3. Locate the front view of the opening ABCE in the roof plane MNOS.

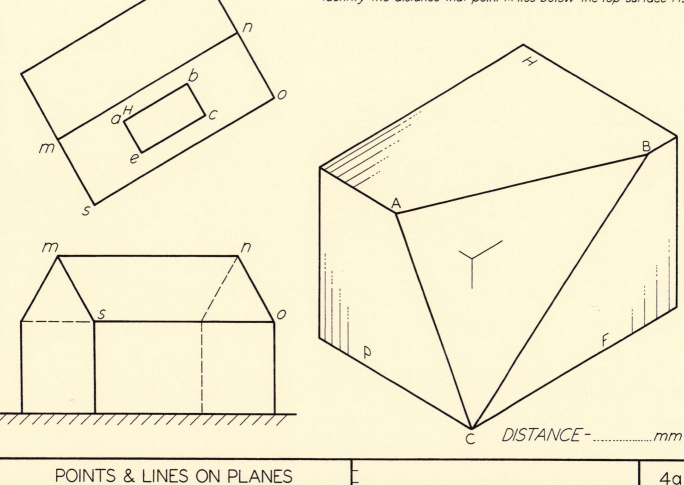

n

b

o

a^H

c

m

e

s

m

n

s

o

4. Locate a point M in plane ABC of the isometric pictorial that lies 16mm from plane F and 10mm to the right of plane P. Identify the distance that point M lies below the top surface H.

H

B

A

P

F

C

DISTANCE-..............mm

POINTS & LINES ON PLANES

4a

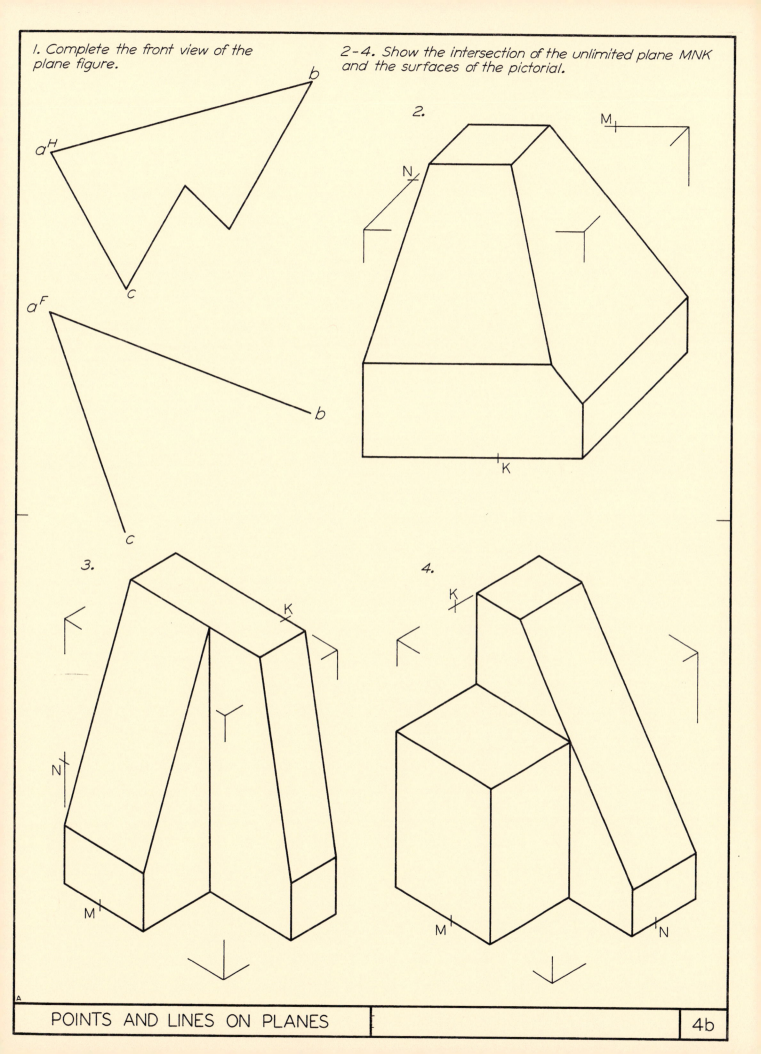

1. Complete the front view of the plane figure.

2-4. Show the intersection of the unlimited plane MNK and the surfaces of the pictorial.

2.

3.

4.

POINTS AND LINES ON PLANES

4b

1. ADD A POINT VIEW OF THE LINE AB.

PROVIDE A POINT VIEW OF LINE AC.

1.

c ——————— a^H

b

b ———————

a^F

c

2. DETERMINE THE MINIMUM CLEARANCE BETWEEN THE THREE 8 mm DIA RODS FOR WHICH THE PARALLEL CENTER-LINES ARE GIVEN.

2.

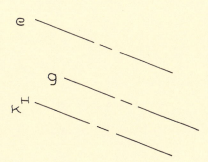

e

g

k^H

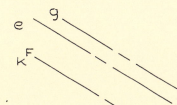

g

e

k^F

3. OBTAIN THE SHORTEST DISTANCE FROM LINE MN TO THE SPHERICAL SURFACE.

3.   DISTANCE   mm

m

+o^H

n

+o^F n

m

4. ADD THE VIEW OF THE PYRAMID THAT SHOWS EDGE AB AS A POINT. PROVIDE A VIEW THAT INCLUDES EDGE VA AS A POINT.

4.

b

a   v^H

c

v^F

a --------- b

c

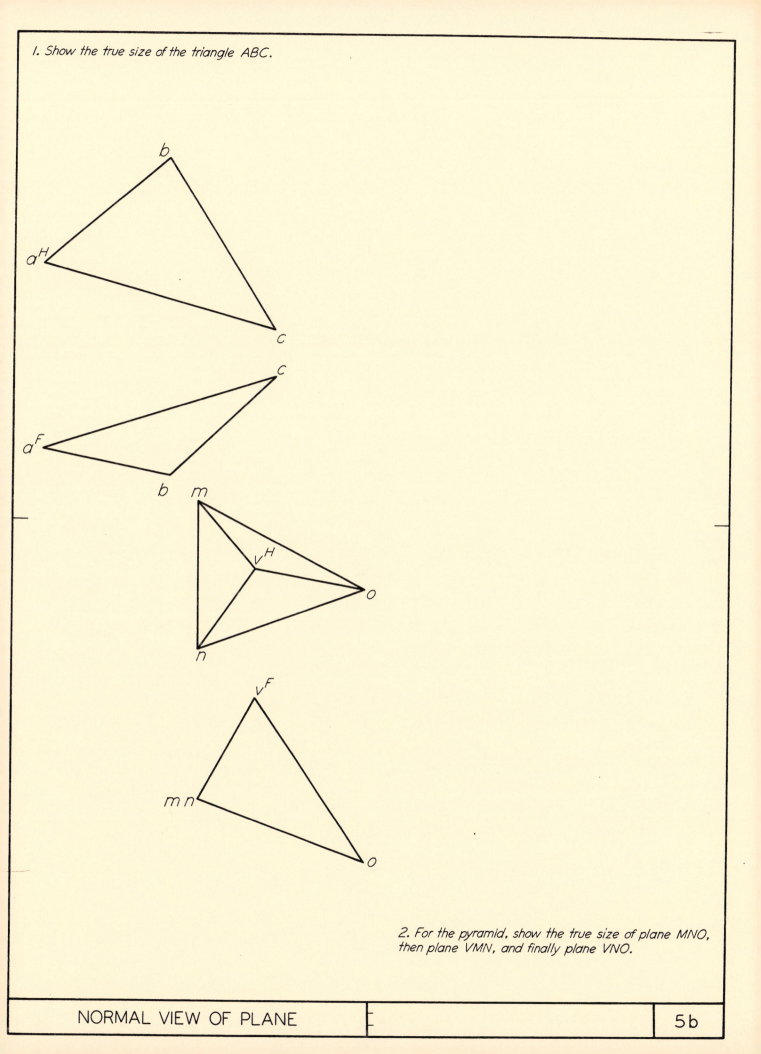

1. Show the true size of the triangle ABC.

b

a^H

c

c

a^F

b m

v^H

o

n

v^F

mn

o

2. For the pyramid, show the true size of plane MNO, then plane VMN, and finally plane VNO.

NORMAL VIEW OF PLANE

5b

On this sheet use the auxiliary-view method and complete the visibility.

1.

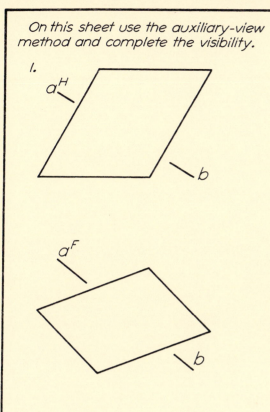

1, 2. Establish the intersection of line AB and the given planes.

2.

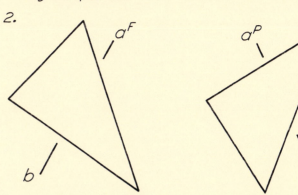

3, 4. Establish the intersection of lines MN and OK with the surfaces of the pyramid.

3.

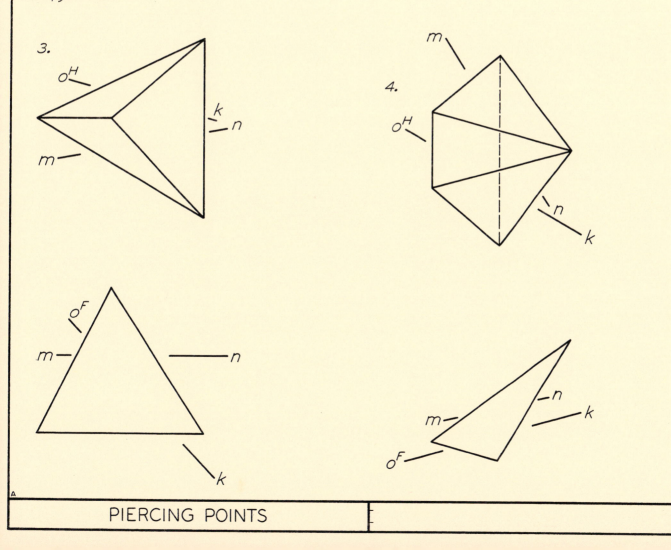

4.

PIERCING POINTS

6a

NOTE: Use the cutting-plane method for these problems.

1, 2. Obtain the intersection of line AB and the plane.

1.

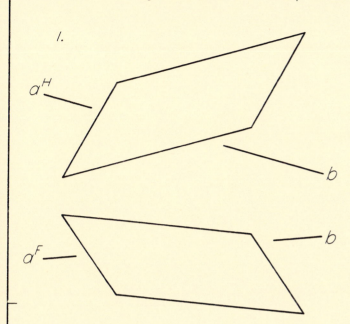

2.

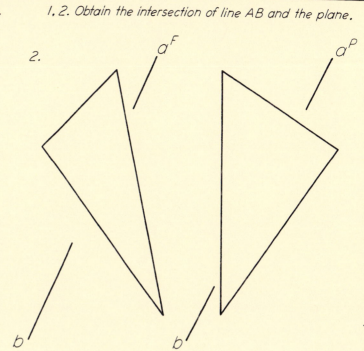

3. Show the intersection of the four frame members with the roof plane.

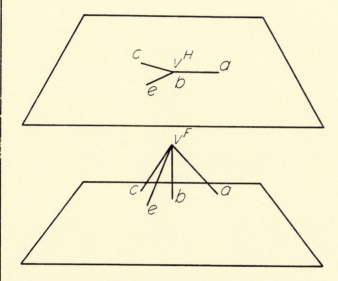

4. Using light source S, obtain the shadow of AB on the plane.

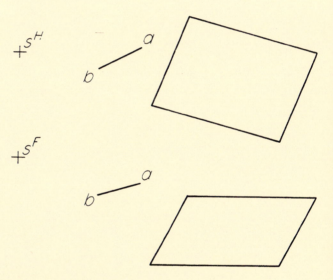

5. Show the intersection of line MN and the pyramidal surfaces.

6. Obtain the intersection of line CE and the hexagonal pyramid.

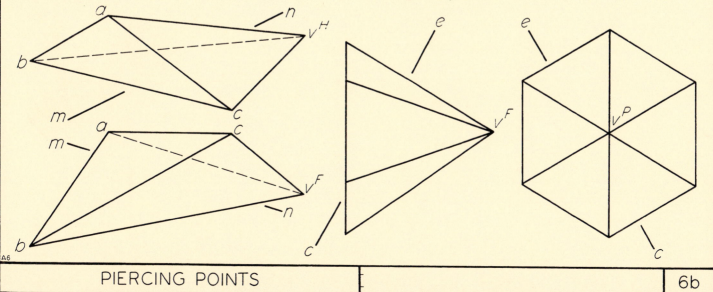

A6

PIERCING POINTS

6b

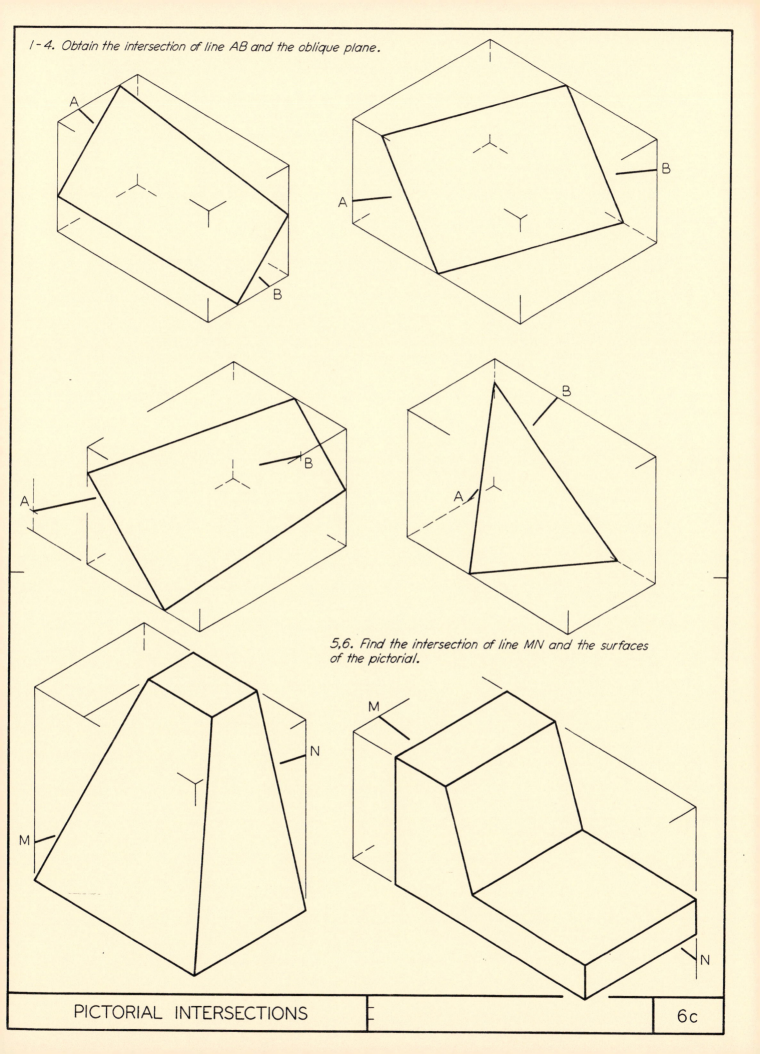

1-4. Obtain the intersection of line AB and the oblique plane.

5,6. Find the intersection of line MN and the surfaces of the pictorial.

PICTORIAL INTERSECTIONS

6c

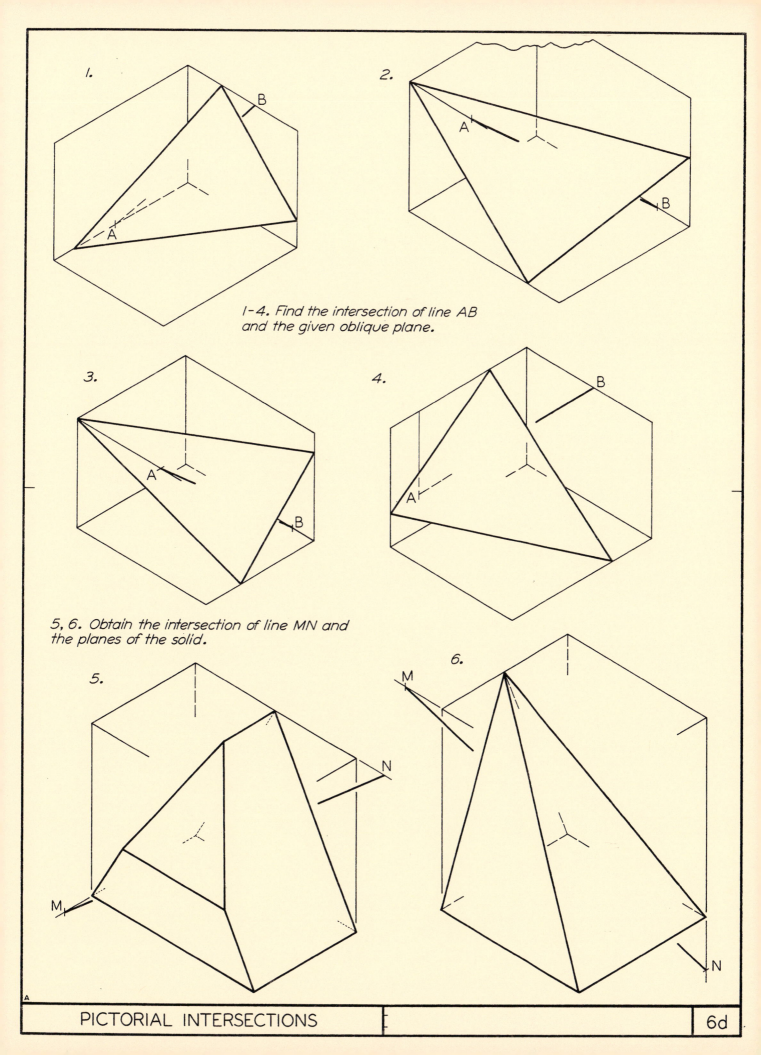

1.

B

A

2.

A

B

1-4. Find the intersection of line AB
and the given oblique plane.

3.

A

B

4.

B

A

5, 6. Obtain the intersection of line MN and
the planes of the solid.

5.

N

M

6.

M

N

PICTORIAL INTERSECTIONS

6d

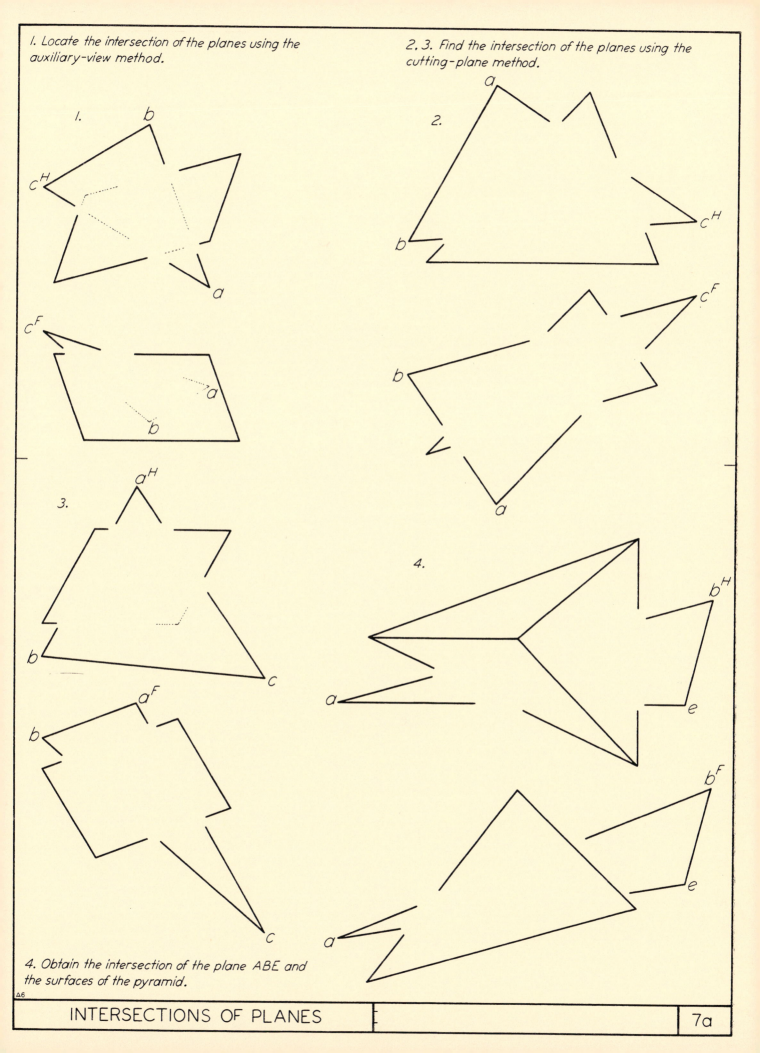

1. Locate the intersection of the planes using the auxiliary-view method.

2, 3. Find the intersection of the planes using the cutting-plane method.

1.

2.

3.

4.

4. Obtain the intersection of the plane ABE and the surfaces of the pyramid.

INTERSECTIONS OF PLANES

7a

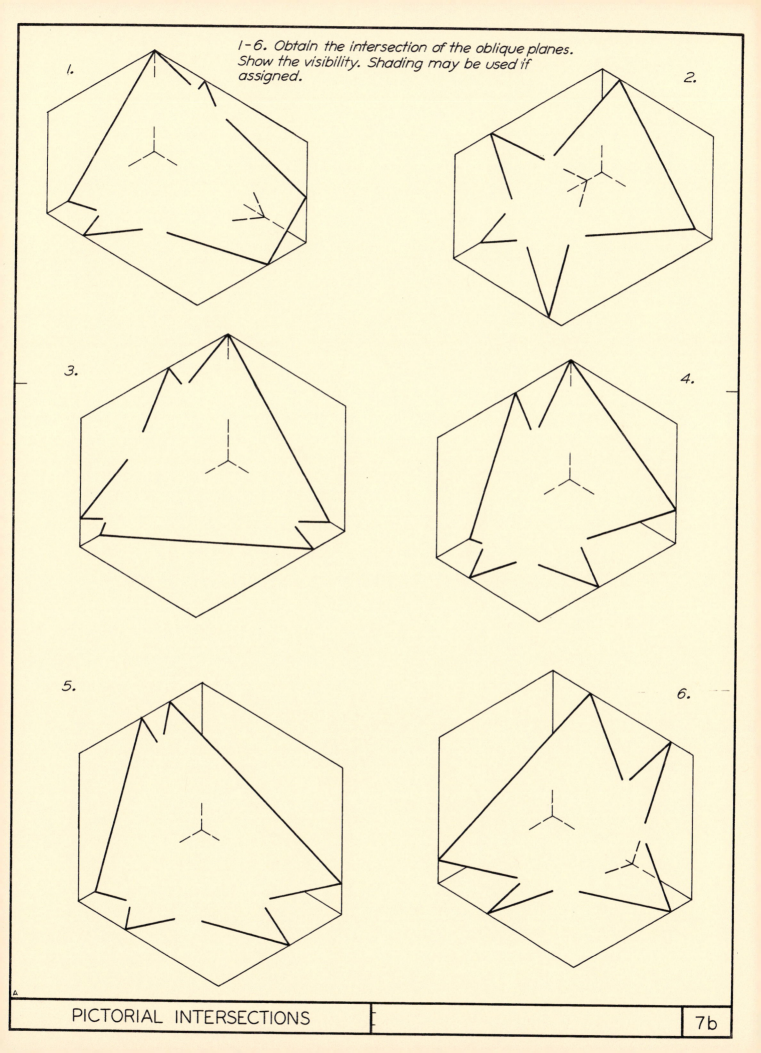

1-6. Obtain the intersection of the oblique planes. Show the visibility. Shading may be used if assigned.

1.

2.

3.

4.

5.

6.

PICTORIAL INTERSECTIONS

7b

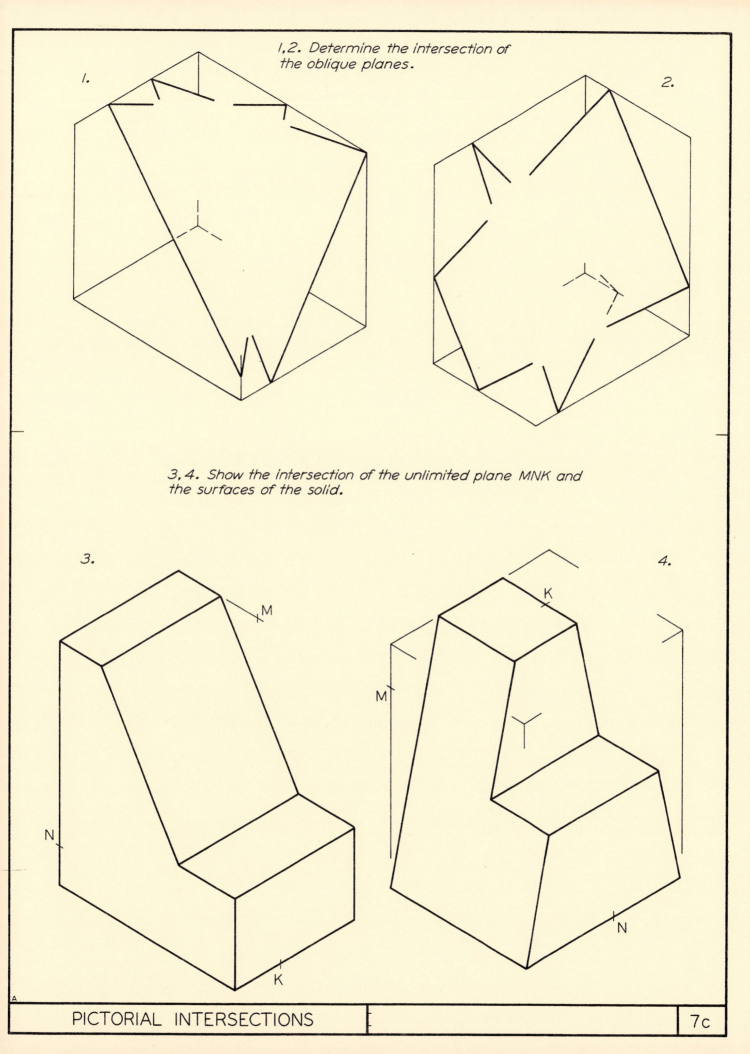

1,2. Determine the intersection of the oblique planes.

1.

2.

3,4. Show the intersection of the unlimited plane MNK and the surfaces of the solid.

3.

M

N

K

4.

K

M

N

PICTORIAL INTERSECTIONS

7c

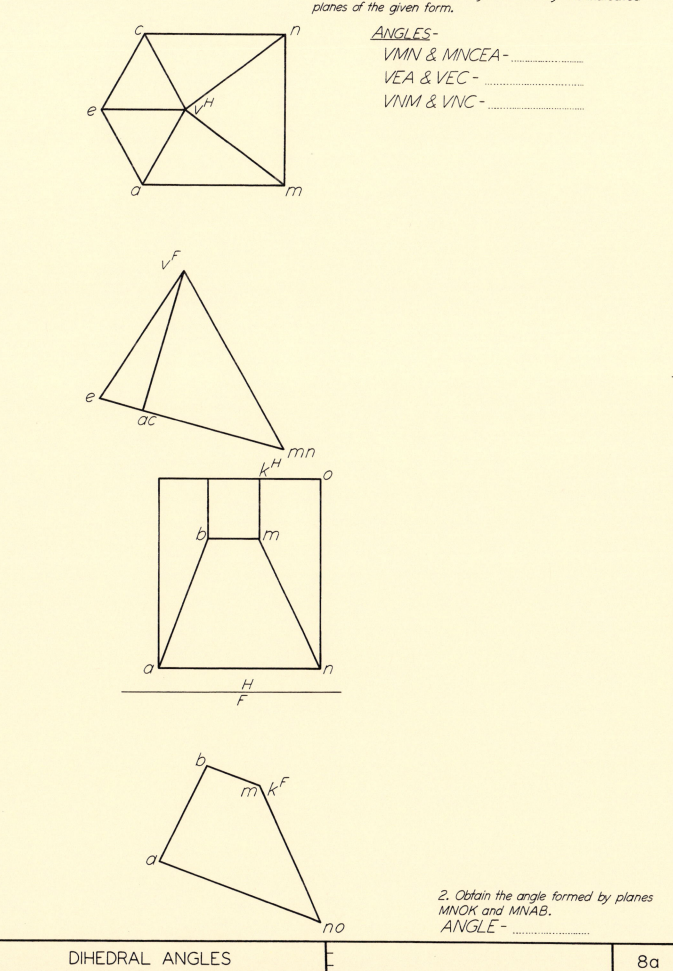

1. Determine the dihedral angles formed by the indicated planes of the given form.

ANGLES-
  VMN & MNCEA - ....
  VEA & VEC - ....
  VNM & VNC - ....

2. Obtain the angle formed by planes MNOK and MNAB.
  ANGLE - ....

DIHEDRAL ANGLES   8a

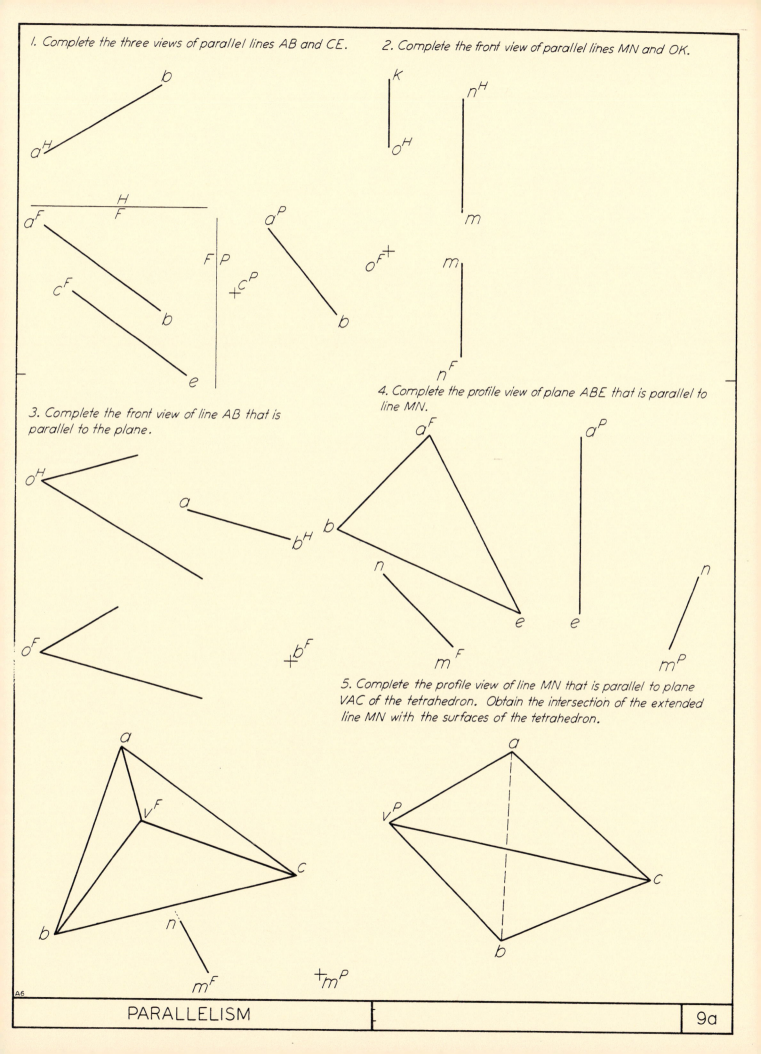

1. Complete the three views of parallel lines AB and CE.

2. Complete the front view of parallel lines MN and OK.

3. Complete the front view of line AB that is parallel to the plane.

4. Complete the profile view of plane ABE that is parallel to line MN.

5. Complete the profile view of line MN that is parallel to plane VAC of the tetrahedron. Obtain the intersection of the extended line MN with the surfaces of the tetrahedron.

A6

PARALLELISM

9a

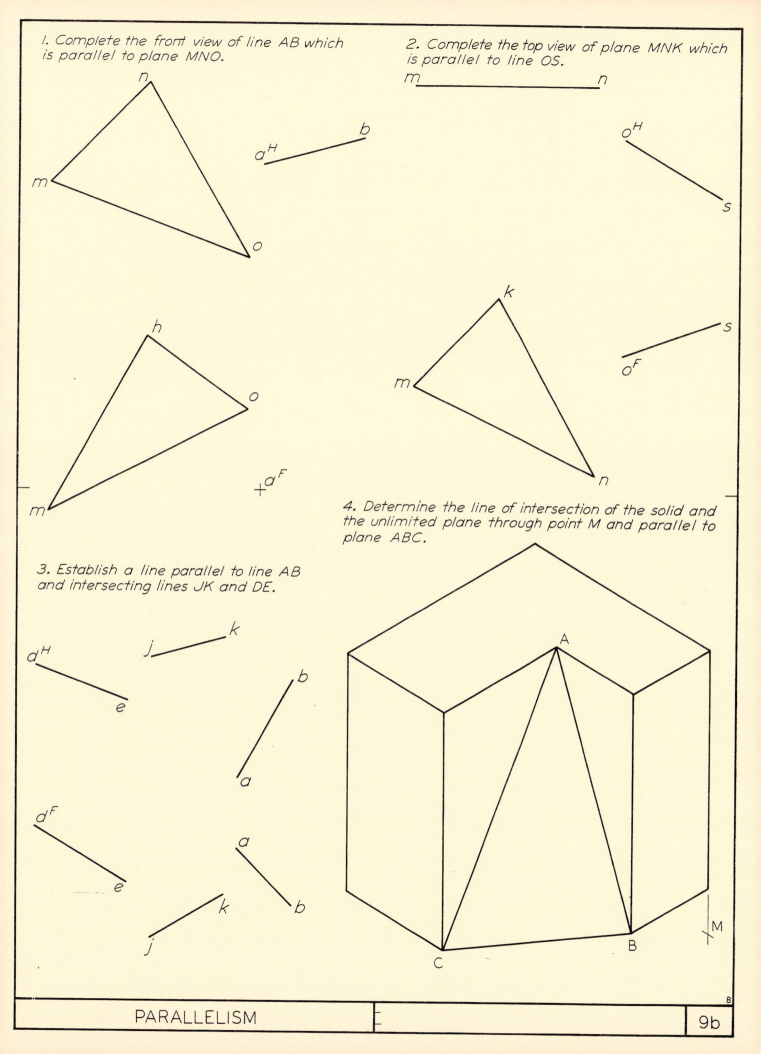

1. Complete the front view of line AB which is parallel to plane MNO.

2. Complete the top view of plane MNK which is parallel to line OS.

3. Establish a line parallel to line AB and intersecting lines JK and DE.

4. Determine the line of intersection of the solid and the unlimited plane through point M and parallel to plane ABC.

PARALLELISM

9b

1. Establish the TL and the top and front views of the altitude of the pyramid with vertex V.

2. From point M on plane VB, add the views of a 25 mm line perpendicular to plane VBC. From point N on plane VAB, add the views a line of any selected length perpendicular to plane VAB.

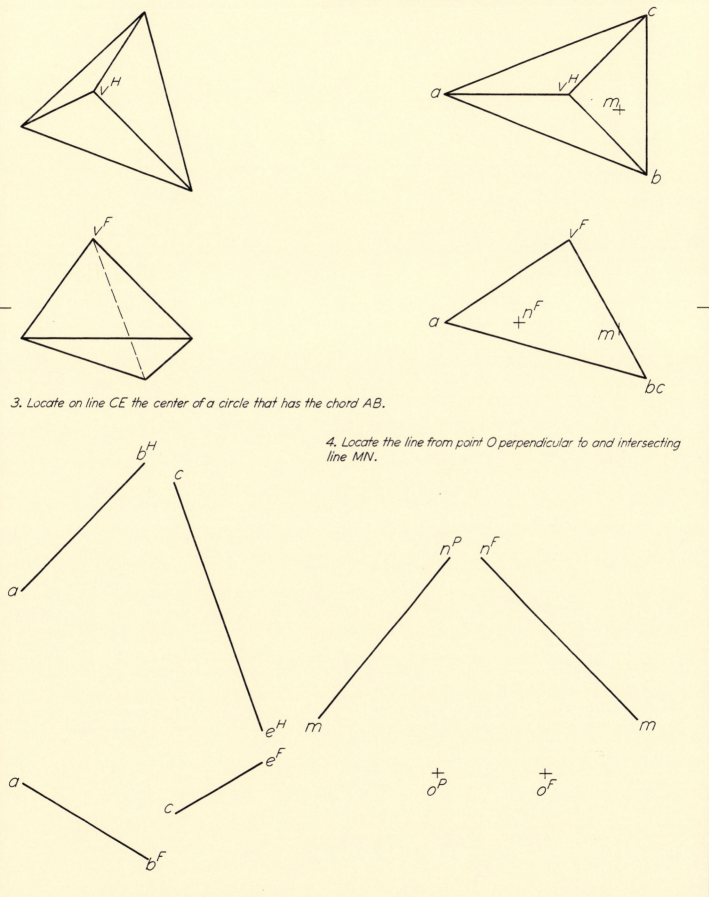

3. Locate on line CE the center of a circle that has the chord AB.

4. Locate the line from point O perpendicular to and intersecting line MN.

PERPENDICULARITY   10a

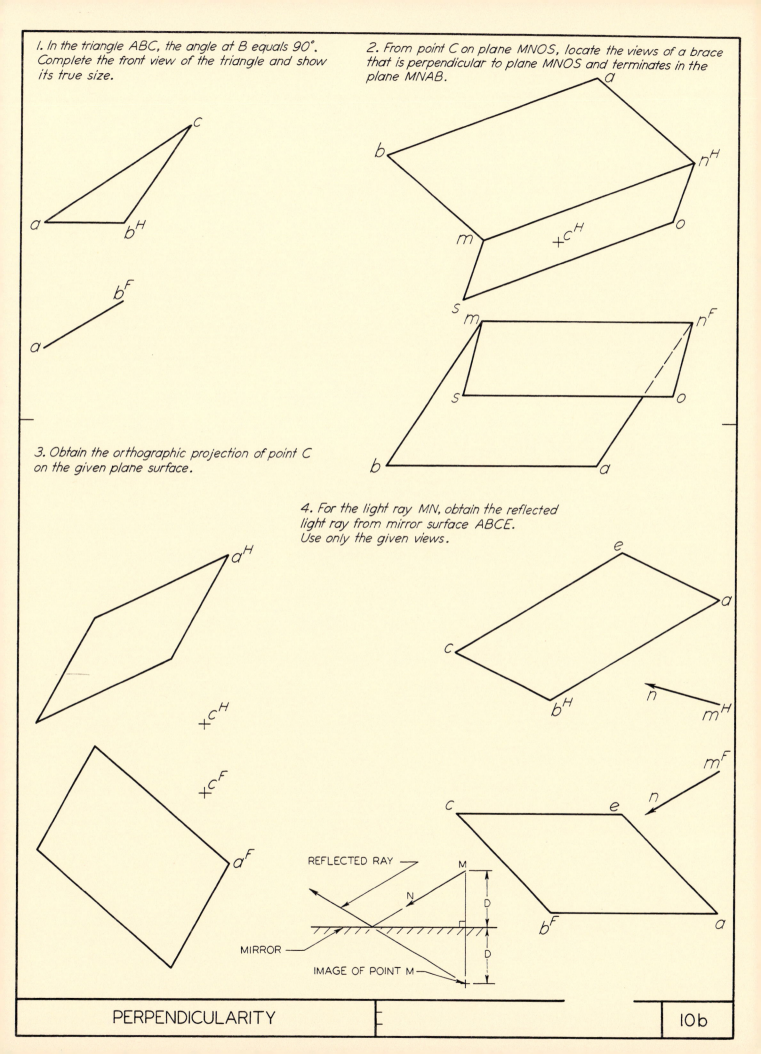

1. In the triangle ABC, the angle at B equals 90°. Complete the front view of the triangle and show its true size.

2. From point C on plane MNOS, locate the views of a brace that is perpendicular to plane MNOS and terminates in the plane MNAB.

3. Obtain the orthographic projection of point C on the given plane surface.

4. For the light ray MN, obtain the reflected light ray from mirror surface ABCE. Use only the given views.

REFLECTED RAY

N

M

D

MIRROR

IMAGE OF POINT M

D

PERPENDICULARITY

10b

I. Show the true length and views of a line representing the shortest distance between the skew lines AB and CE.

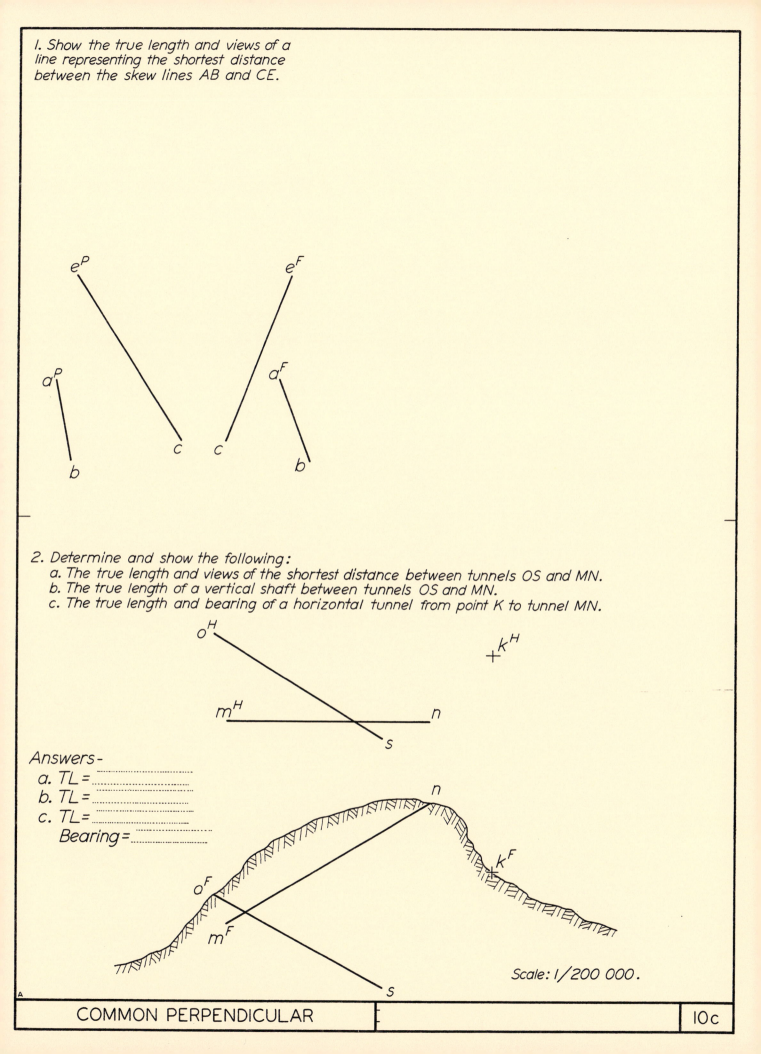

eᴾ

eᶠ

aᴾ

aᶠ

c

c

b

b

2. Determine and show the following:
   a. The true length and views of the shortest distance between tunnels OS and MN.
   b. The true length of a vertical shaft between tunnels OS and MN.
   c. The true length and bearing of a horizontal tunnel from point K to tunnel MN.

oᴴ

+kᴴ

mᴴ

n

s

Answers-
   a. TL = ...
   b. TL = ...
   c. TL = ...
      Bearing = ...

n

oᶠ

kᶠ

mᶠ

s

Scale: 1/200 000.

COMMON PERPENDICULAR

10c

1. Obtain the true angle between line AB and the given plane.

ANGLE = ...

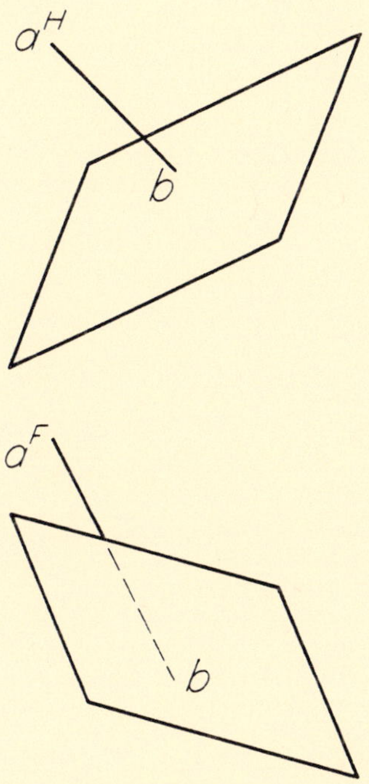

a^H
b
a^F
b

2a. Show the true angle formed by line VA and the plane ABC.
b. Obtain the true angle formed by line VB and plane ABC.

ANGLES - VA-ABC = ..., VA-ABC = ...

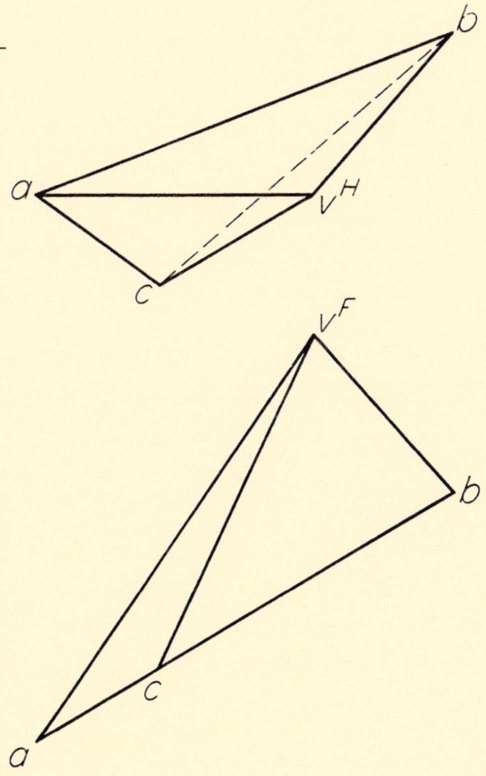

b
a
v^H
c
v^F
b
c
a

A6

ANGLE BETWEEN LINE & PLANE		11a

1. Secure the strike and dip of the plane ABC.

STRIKE-...................................

DIP-...................................

2. Points M, N, and O are on the upper bedding plane of an ore vein. Obtain the strike and dip of the vein. Point E is on the parallel lower bedding plane. Find the thickness of the vein. Scale: 1/1000.

STRIKE-........................., DIP-...........................

THICKNESS-...........................

$+m$

o_+

a^H

c

b

e^H+ $+n^H$

a^F

b

c

$+n^F$

$+e^F$

$+m$

$+o$

3. Locate the front view of point C in the upper bedding plane ABC of the vein that has a dip of 35°SE. Find the top view of point K that is in the lower bedding plane of this 8 meter-thick ore vein.

b^H_+

a^H_+

$+c^H$

a^F+

b^F+

k^F+

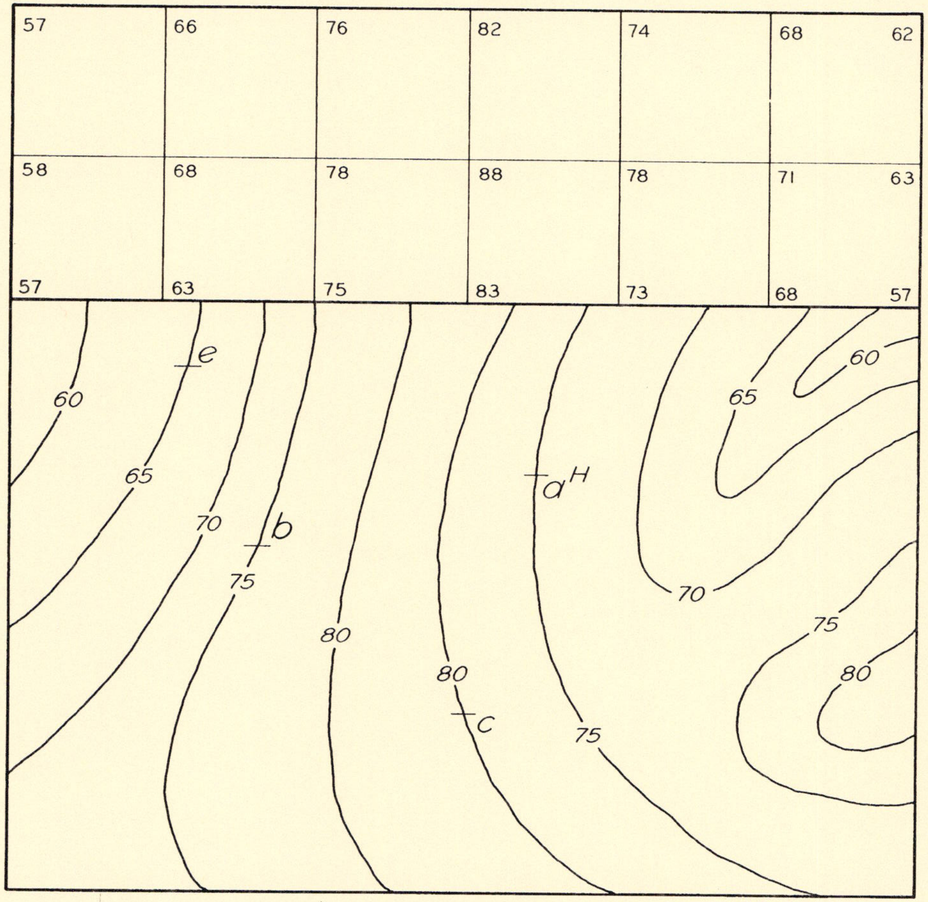

Scale 1:500
(Contour lines in meters.)

1. Given points A, B, and C on the upper outcrop line of a vein and point E on the lower outcrop line, find the strike, dip, and thickness of the vein.
2. Plot the contour lines for the adjacent property for which the results of a grid survey are indicated.
3. Locate the outcrop lines in both areas.

Strike = ...   Dip = ...   Thickness = ...

CONTOUR MAP AND OUTCROP

12b

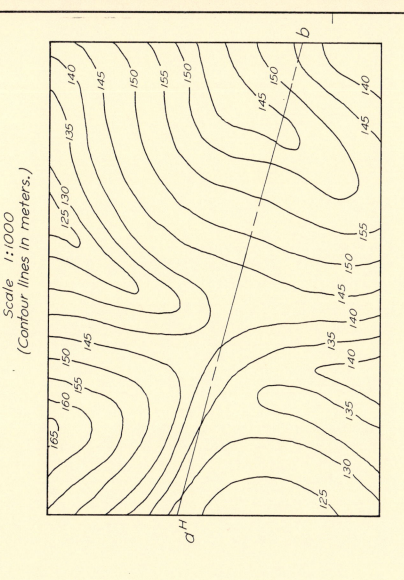

Scale 1:1000
(Contour lines in meters.)

Line AB is the centerline of a 20m wide roadway that has a constant elevation of 140 meters.

1. Plot the elevation view of the profile of the center line.
2. Plot the lines of cut and fill (in the map) if the cut is to be made at a 1 to 1 slope and the fill at a 1 to 2 slope as illustrated below. Identify the areas by shading as indicated.

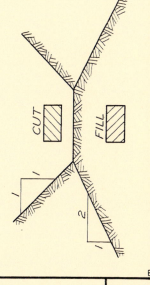

CUT AND FILL FOR ROADWAY

12 c

B

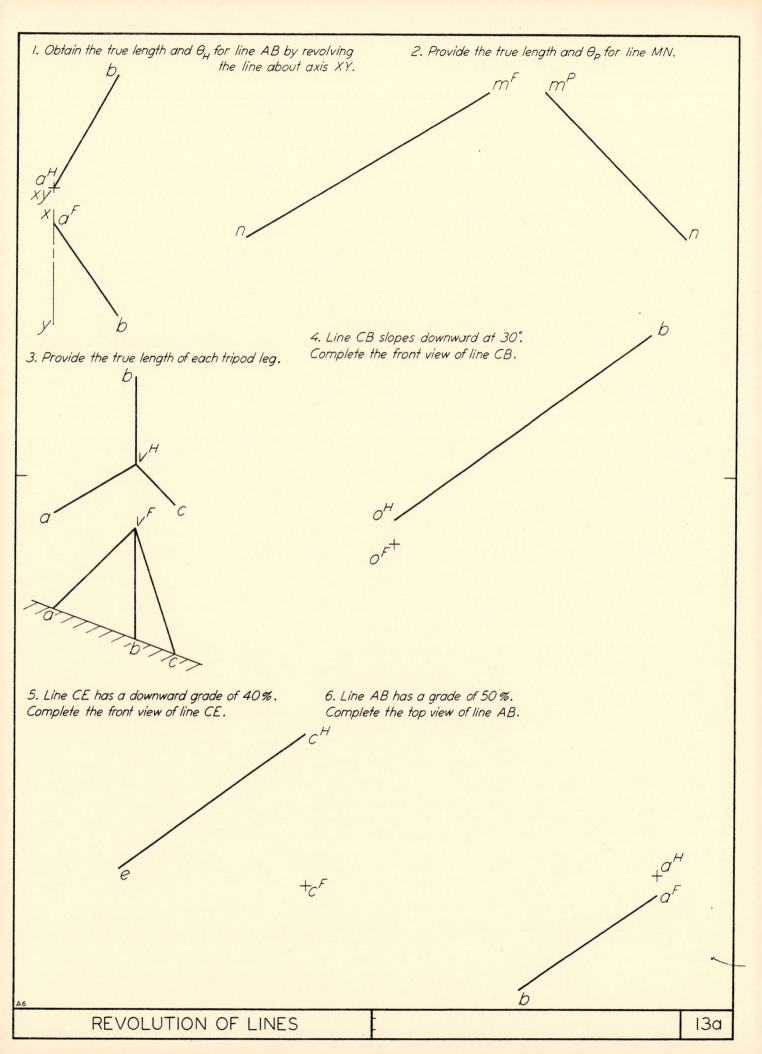

1. Obtain the true length and θ_H for line AB by revolving the line about axis XY.

b

a^H
XY
X a^F

y   b

2. Provide the true length and θ_P for line MN.

m^F   m^P

n   n

3. Provide the true length of each tripod leg.

b

v^H

a   c

v^F

a   b   c

4. Line CB slopes downward at 30°. Complete the front view of line CB.

b

o^H

o^F

5. Line CE has a downward grade of 40%. Complete the front view of line CE.

c^H

e

+c^F

6. Line AB has a grade of 50%. Complete the top view of line AB.

+a^H
a^F

b

A6

REVOLUTION OF LINES   13a

1. Forces A and B are in a frontal plane. Find their resultant and determine the force component tending to lift the point of application. Start the force polygon at point O and layout the forces in alphabetical order. Scale: 1mm/20N.

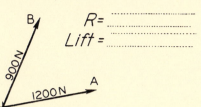

R= ....
Lift = ...

Not to scale.

o_{+}^{F}

2. Forces E, F, and G are in a frontal plane. Find their resultant and determine the force component tending to cause the anchor to slide. Start the polygon at point P. Scale: 1mm/20N.

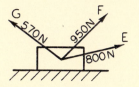

R = ...
S.C. = ...

p_{+}^{F}

3. Determine the forces in members M and N when they are acted upon by the 150 kg mass hanging from point K. Start the force polygon at point Q. Scale: 1mm/20N.

q_{+}^{F}

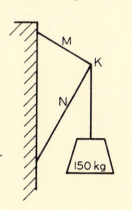

4. To pull a car from a soft shoulder, one end of a rope is tied to the car and the other end is tied to a post. A 450 N force applied at point S creates what tension in the rope tending to move the car? Start the force polygon at point T. Scale: 1mm/20N.

Force = ...

t_{+}^{H}

m_{+}^{H}

Force in M = ...

Force in N = ...

n_{+}^{H}

Distance = ...   Time = ...

5. A ship at point M is following a course of N-120° at 12.1 knots. A ship at point N is on a course of N-135° at 6.8 knots. How close will the ships pass? How much time will elapse before this situation occurs? Vector Scale: 1cm/2 knots.   Distance Scale: 1/10 000.

1. Find the H and F projections and the true magnitude
of the resultant of the three forces A, B, and C.
Complete the parallelepiped using line weights
similar to those in the pictorial.
Scale: 1mm / 10N.

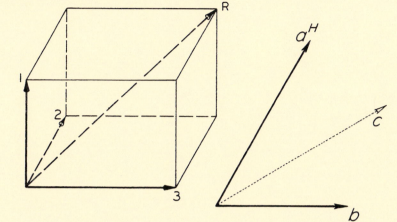

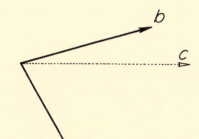

$R=$ ....

2. Resolve the given vector R into com-
ponents along the members D, E, and F.

d^P d^F

e e

f f

1. Find the magnitude and sense of the resultant (R) of the four vectors A, B, C, and D.
   Start the Space Diagram at point X.   Scale: 1mm = 10 N

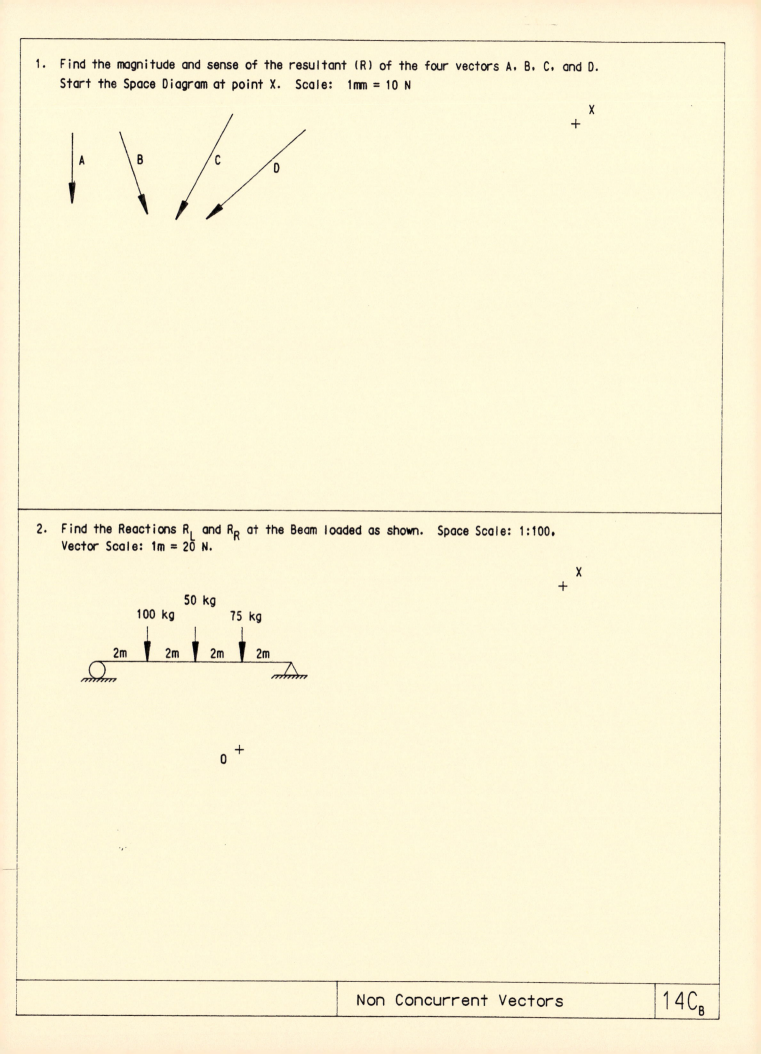

X
+

A   B   C
              D

2. Find the Reactions R_L and R_R at the Beam loaded as shown.   Space Scale: 1:100,
   Vector Scale: 1m = 20 N.

X
+

50 kg
100 kg   75 kg

2m   2m   2m   2m

0 +

Non Concurrent Vectors $14C_B$

1. Find the Reactions R_L and R_R of the Truss. Find the loads in each member of the Truss.
    Locate the start of the Stress Diagram and Vector Diagram at X. Scales:

X
+

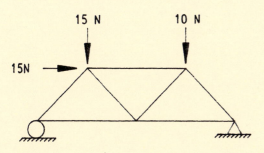

15 N   10 N

15N →

2.   Scale:

X
+

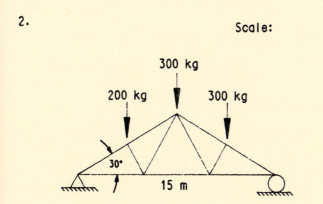

300 kg

200 kg   300 kg

30°

15 m

| | Truss Stresses | $14D_B$ |

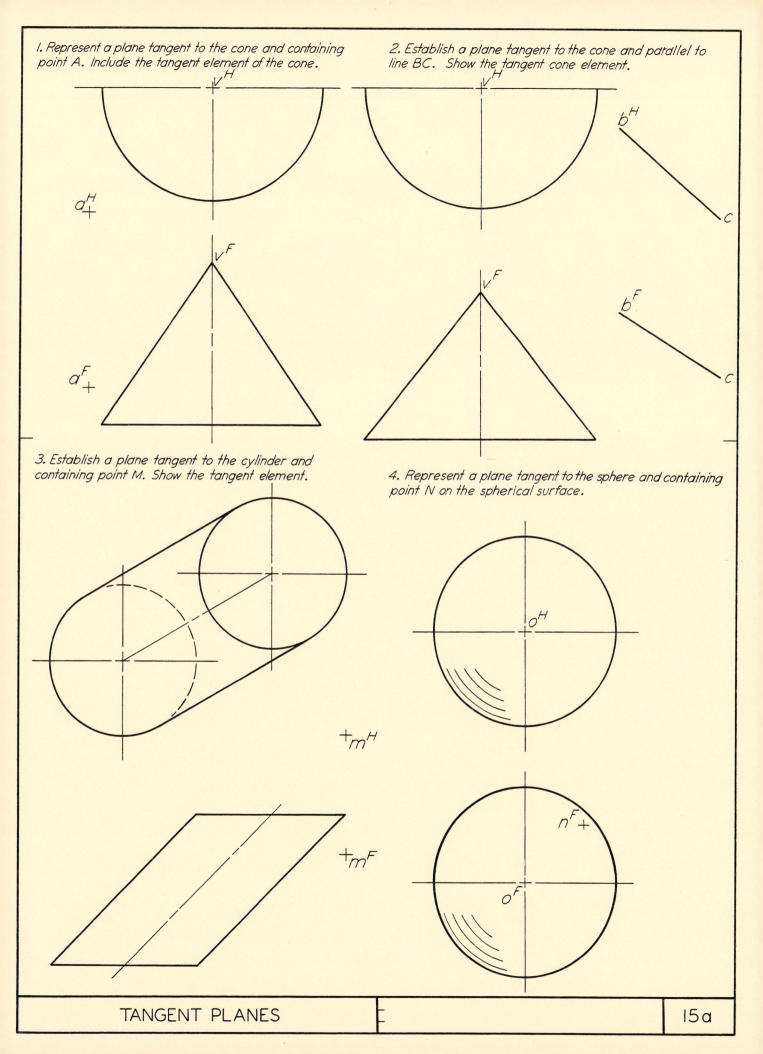

1. Represent a plane tangent to the cone and containing point A. Include the tangent element of the cone.

V^H

a^H_+

V^F

a^F_+

2. Establish a plane tangent to the cone and parallel to line BC. Show the tangent cone element.

V^H

b^H

c

V^F

b^F

c

3. Establish a plane tangent to the cylinder and containing point M. Show the tangent element.

$+m^H$

$+m^F$

4. Represent a plane tangent to the sphere and containing point N on the spherical surface.

o^H

n^F+

o^F

TANGENT PLANES

15a

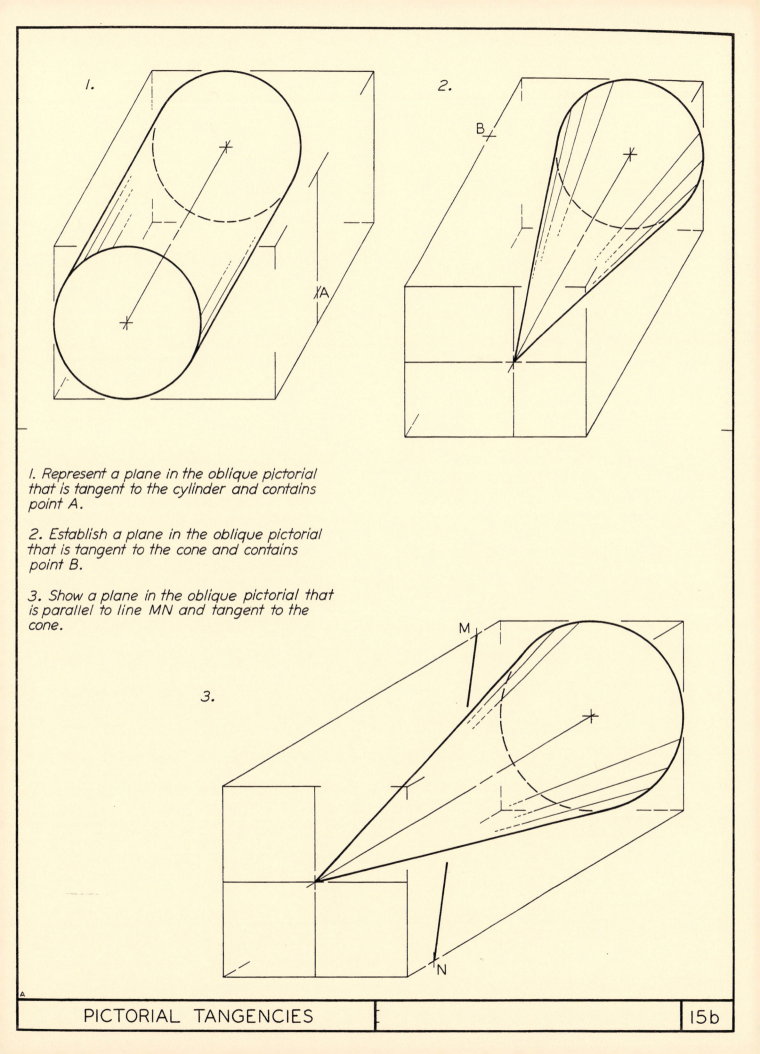

1. Represent a plane in the oblique pictorial that is tangent to the cylinder and contains point A.

2. Establish a plane in the oblique pictorial that is tangent to the cone and contains point B.

3. Show a plane in the oblique pictorial that is parallel to line MN and tangent to the cone.

PICTORIAL TANGENCIES

15b

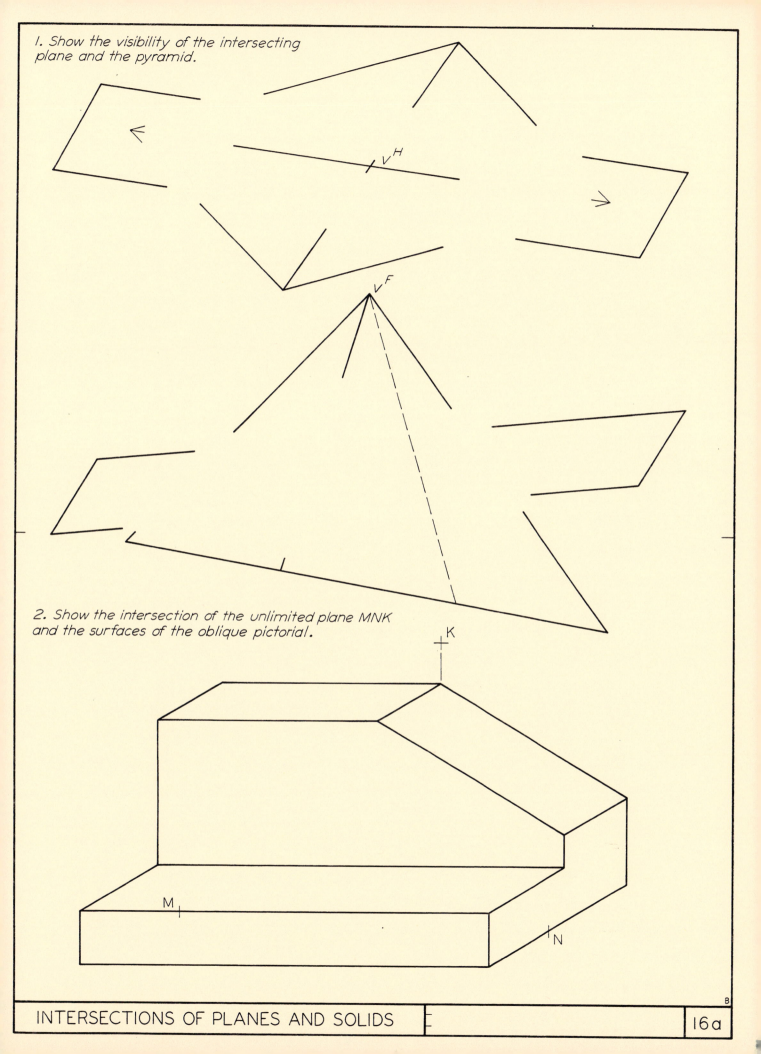

1. Show the visibility of the intersecting
plane and the pyramid.

V^H

V^F

2. Show the intersection of the unlimited plane MNK
and the surfaces of the oblique pictorial.

K

M

N

INTERSECTIONS OF PLANES AND SOLIDS

16a

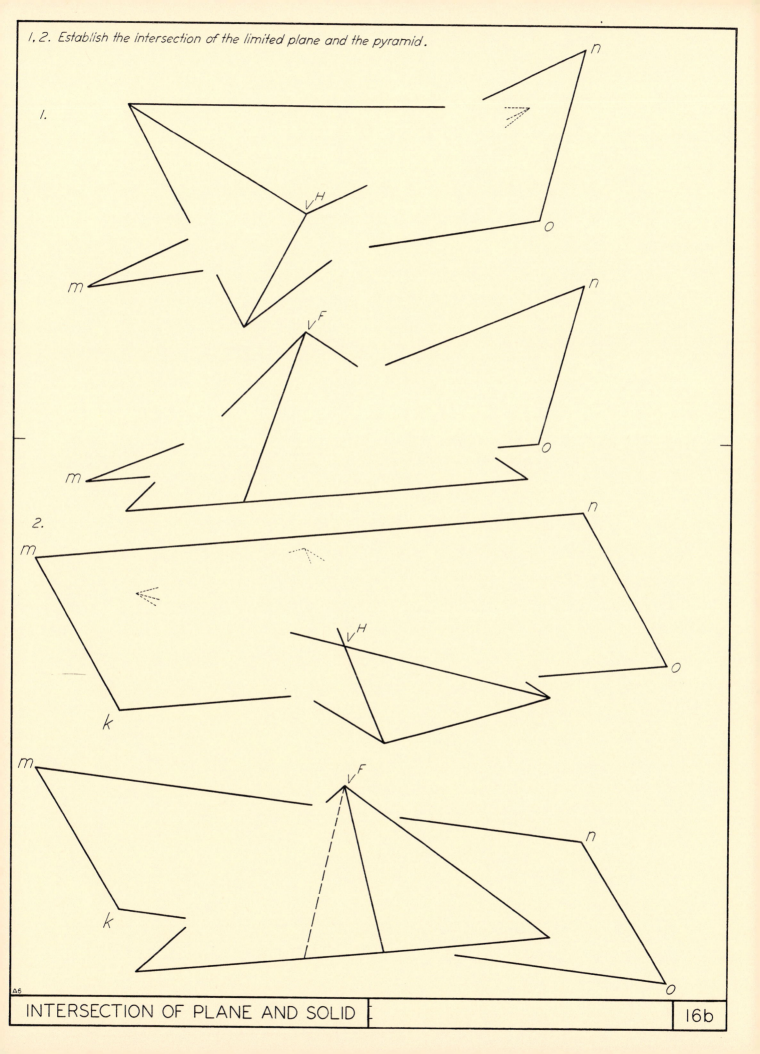

INTERSECTION OF PLANE AND SOLID

16b

Develop the pyramidal portion
of the sheet metal hopper. Start
the development as indicated
below.

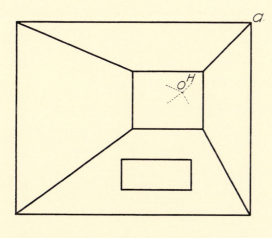

<u>HOPPER</u>
for dust collector unit

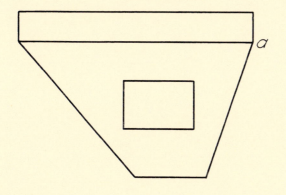

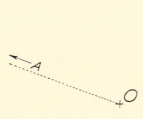

RADIAL LINE DEVELOPMENT

17a

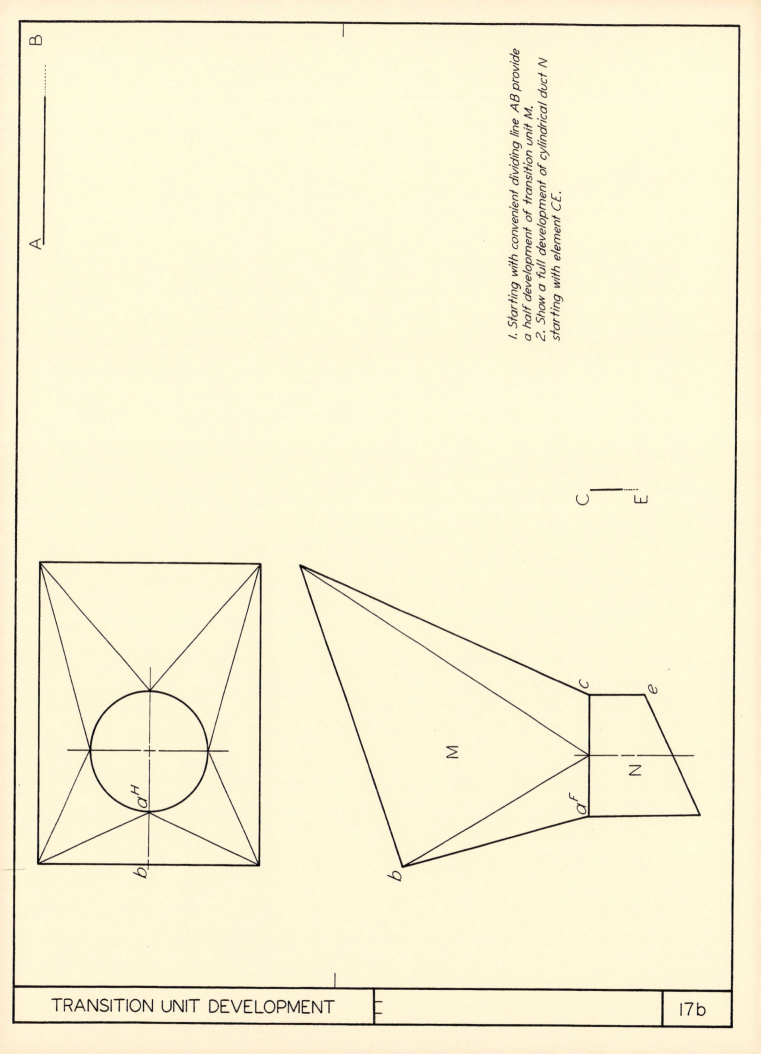

B ⸺⸺ A

1. Starting with convenient dividing line AB provide a half development of transition unit M.
2. Show a full development of cylindrical duct N starting with element CE.

C ⸺
E ⸺

a^H b

M

a^F b   c   e

N

TRANSITION UNIT DEVELOPMENT   17b

Establish the lines of intersection of the pyramid and the prism.

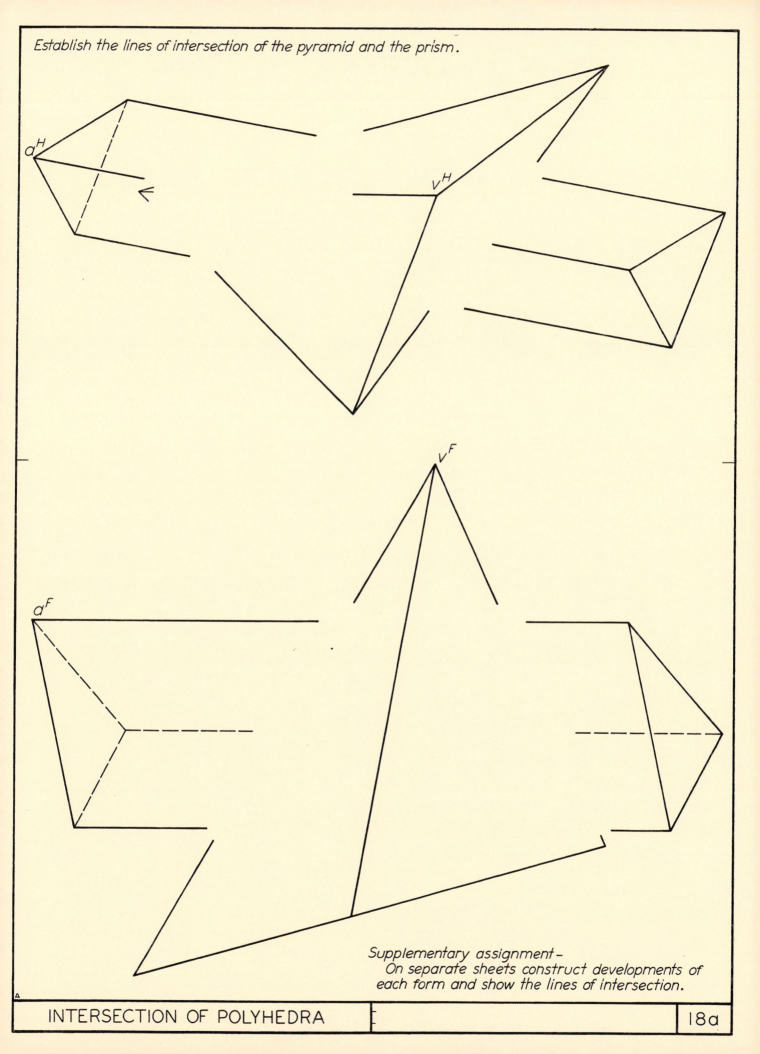

Obtain the intersection of the prism and cone, and the
cylinder and cone.

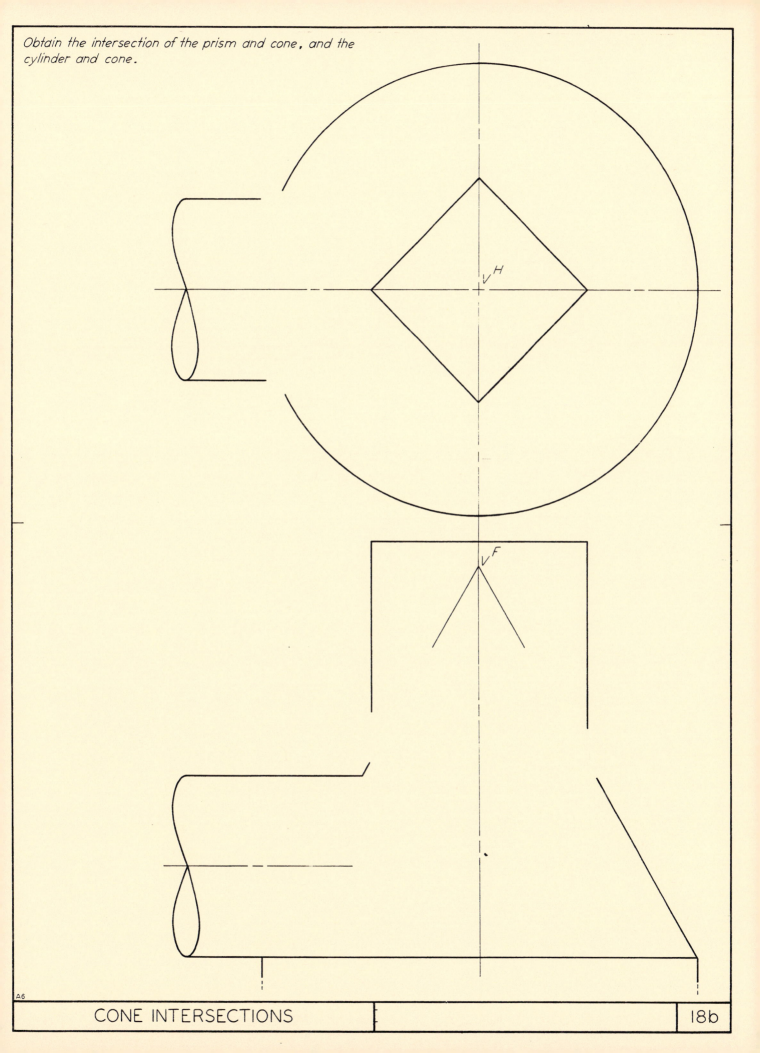

V^H

V^F

A6

CONE INTERSECTIONS   18b

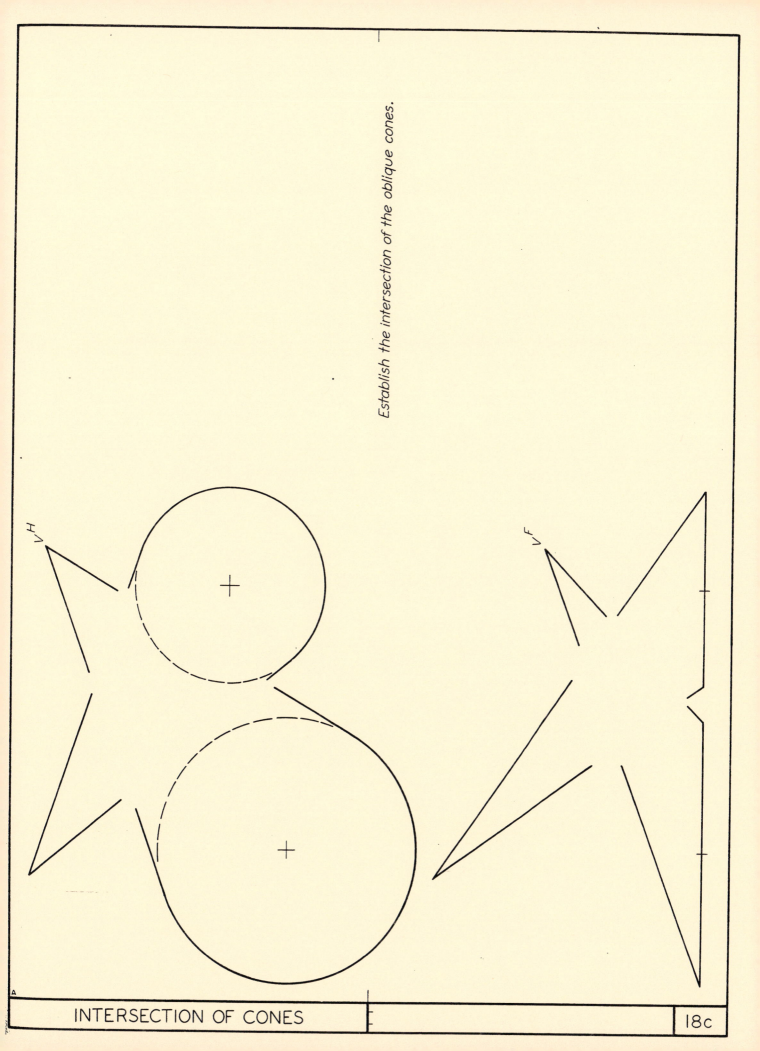

Establish the intersection of the oblique cones.

V H

V F

INTERSECTION OF CONES

18c

Show the complete shade and shadow of the
house, garage, and chimney.

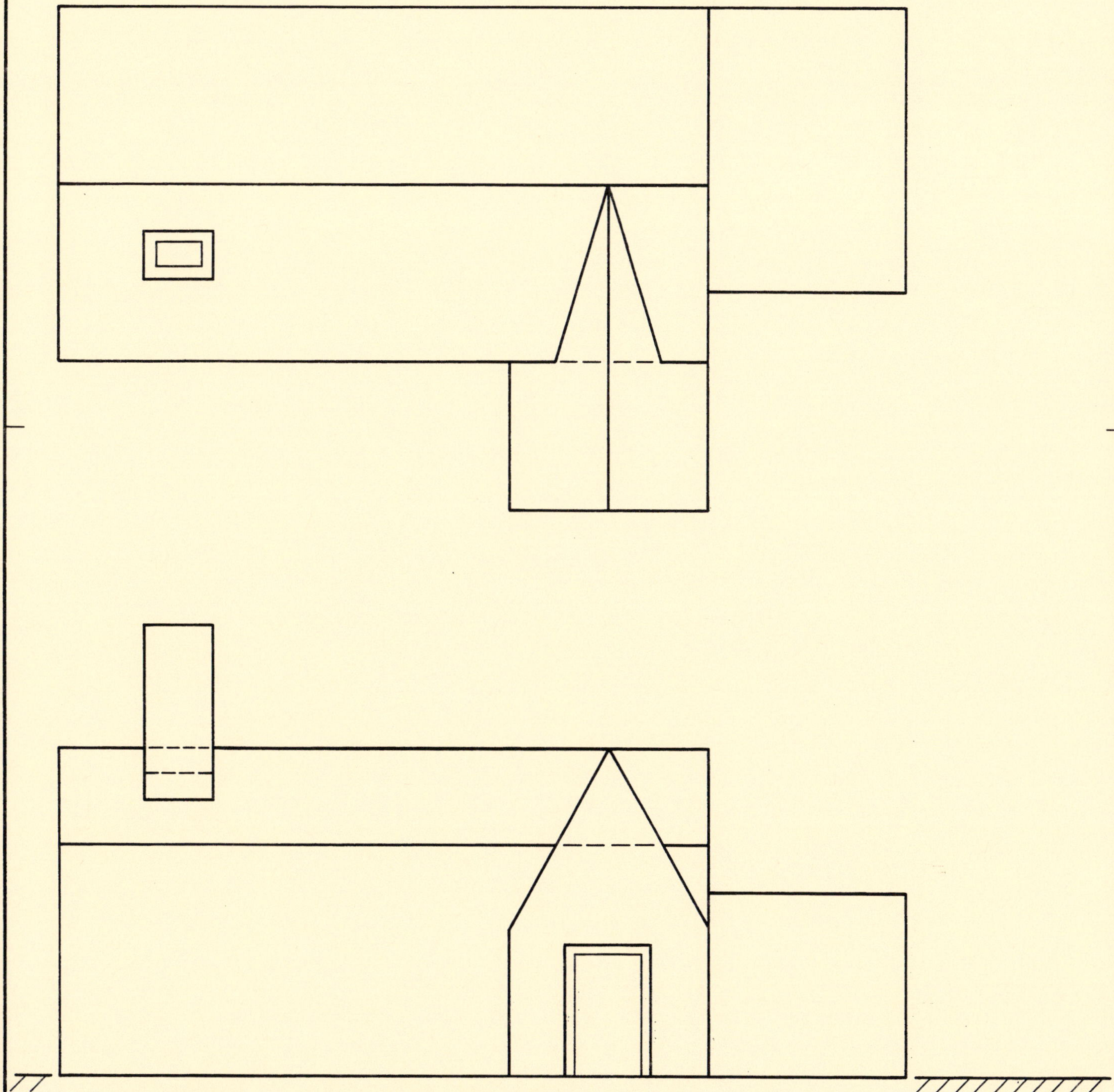

19a

SHADE AND SHADOW

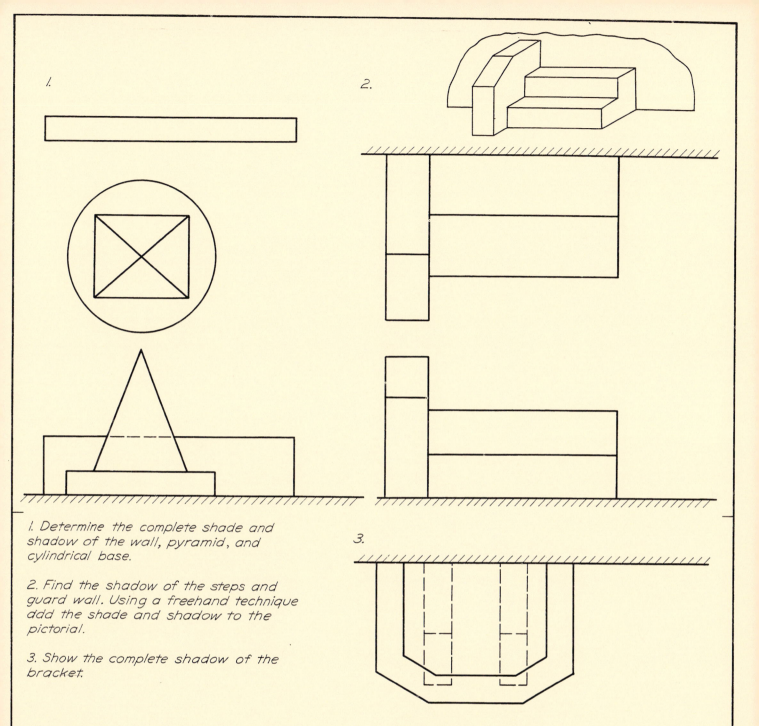

1.

2.

1. Determine the complete shade and shadow of the wall, pyramid, and cylindrical base.

2. Find the shadow of the steps and guard wall. Using a freehand technique add the shade and shadow to the pictorial.

3. Show the complete shadow of the bracket.

3.

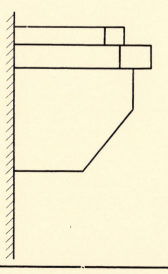

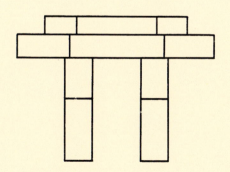

SHADES AND SHADOWS

B

19b

1. 2. Provide the shade and shadow for each pictorial.

1.

2.

A

B

LIGHT RAY
DIRECTION

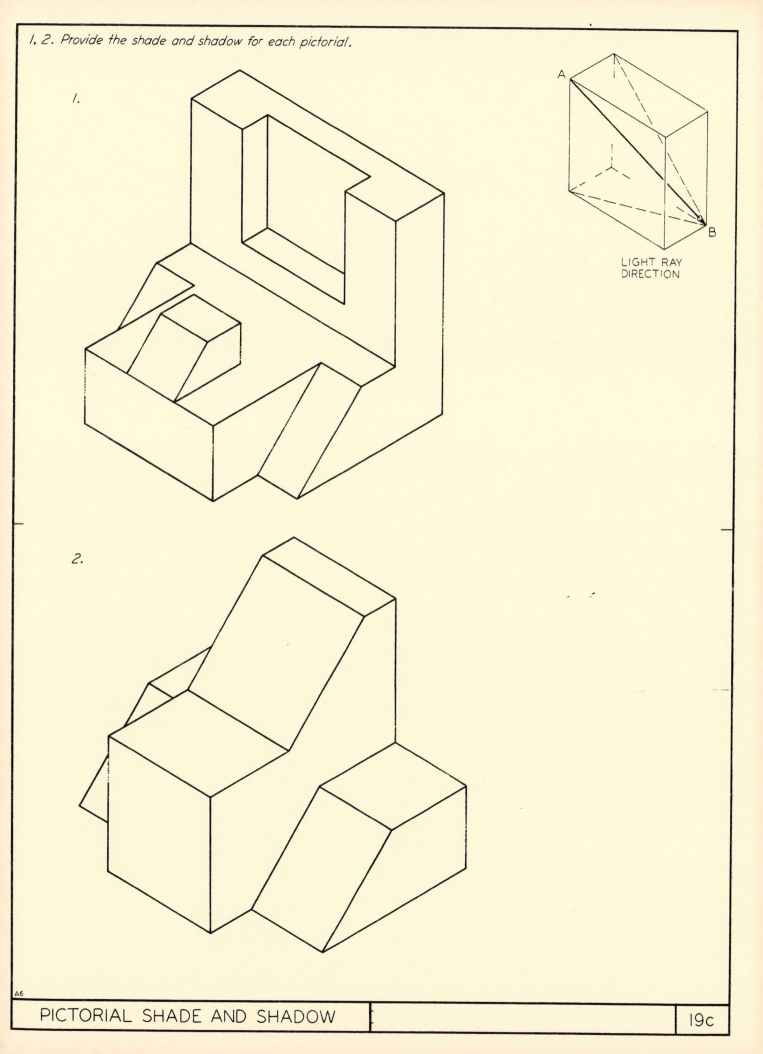

A6

PICTORIAL SHADE AND SHADOW

19c

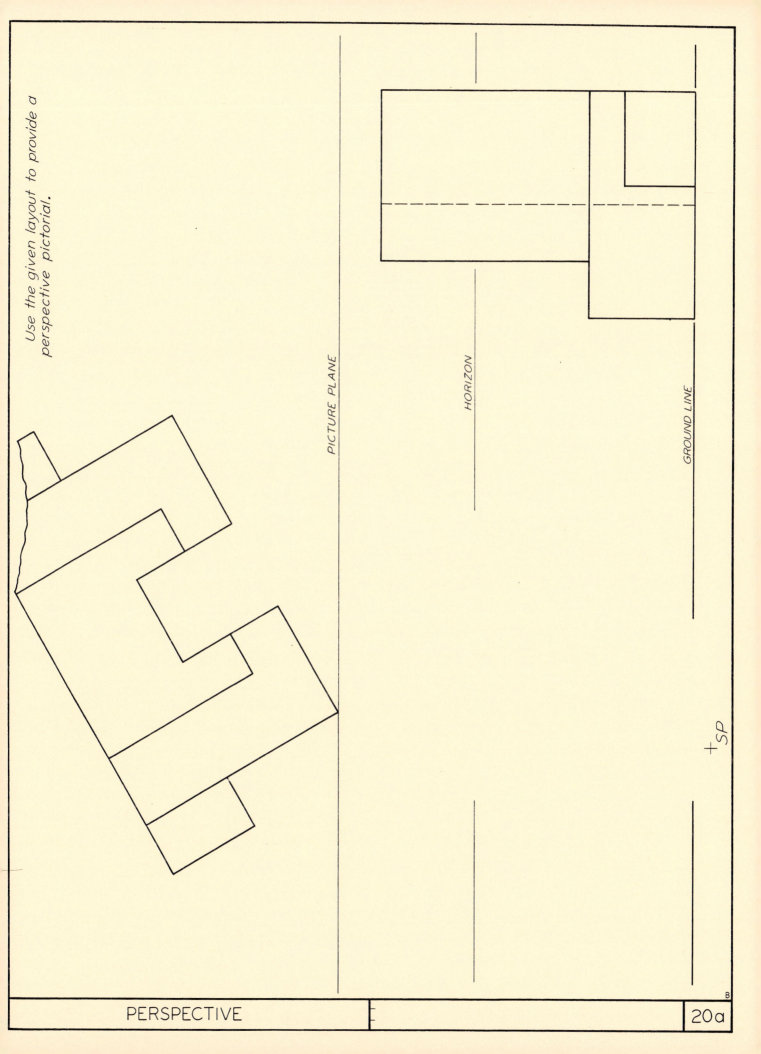

Use the given layout to provide a perspective pictorial.

PICTURE PLANE

HORIZON

GROUND LINE

+ SP

PERSPECTIVE

20a

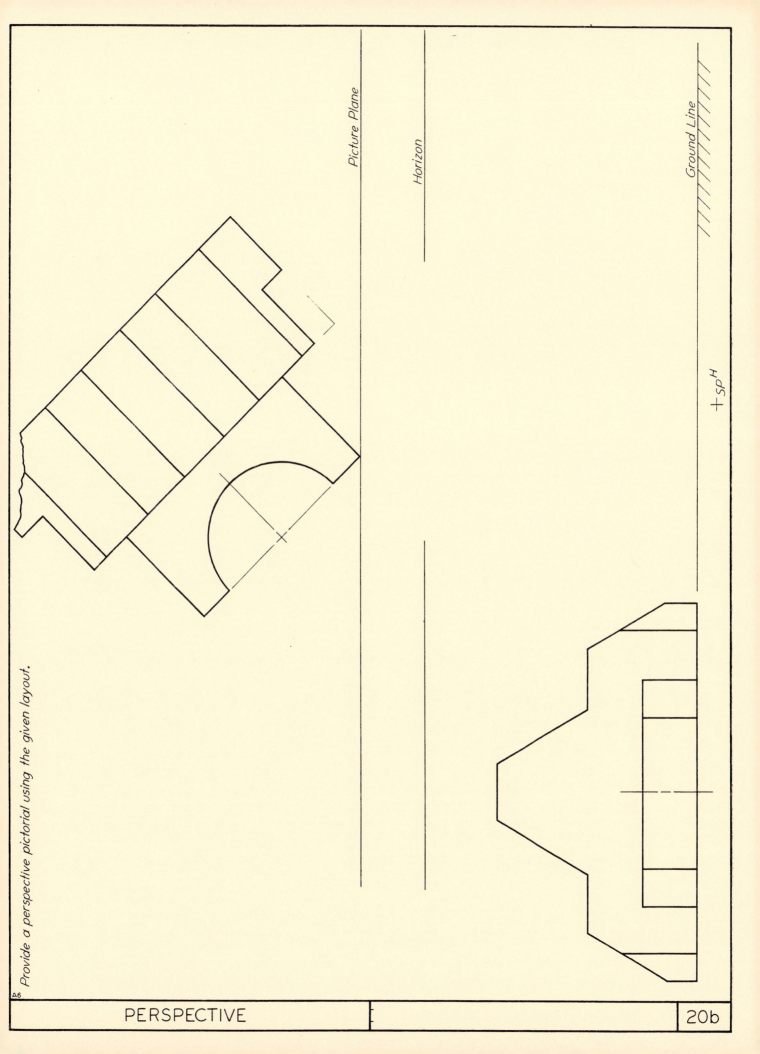

Provide a perspective pictorial using the given layout.

Picture Plane

Horizon

Ground Line

+ SP^H

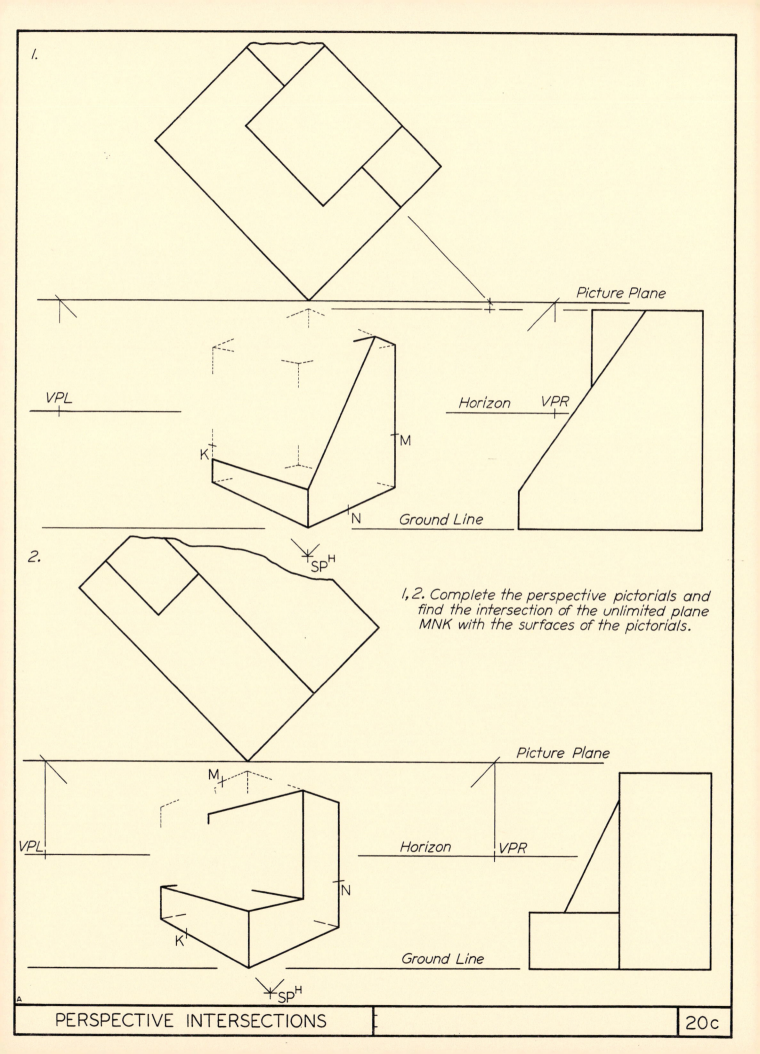

1.

Picture Plane

VPL

Horizon   VPR

M

K

N   Ground Line

SP^H

2.

1, 2. Complete the perspective pictorials and
find the intersection of the unlimited plane
MNK with the surfaces of the pictorials.

Picture Plane

M

Horizon   VPR

VPL

N

K

Ground Line

SP^H

PERSICTIVE INTERSECTIONS   20c

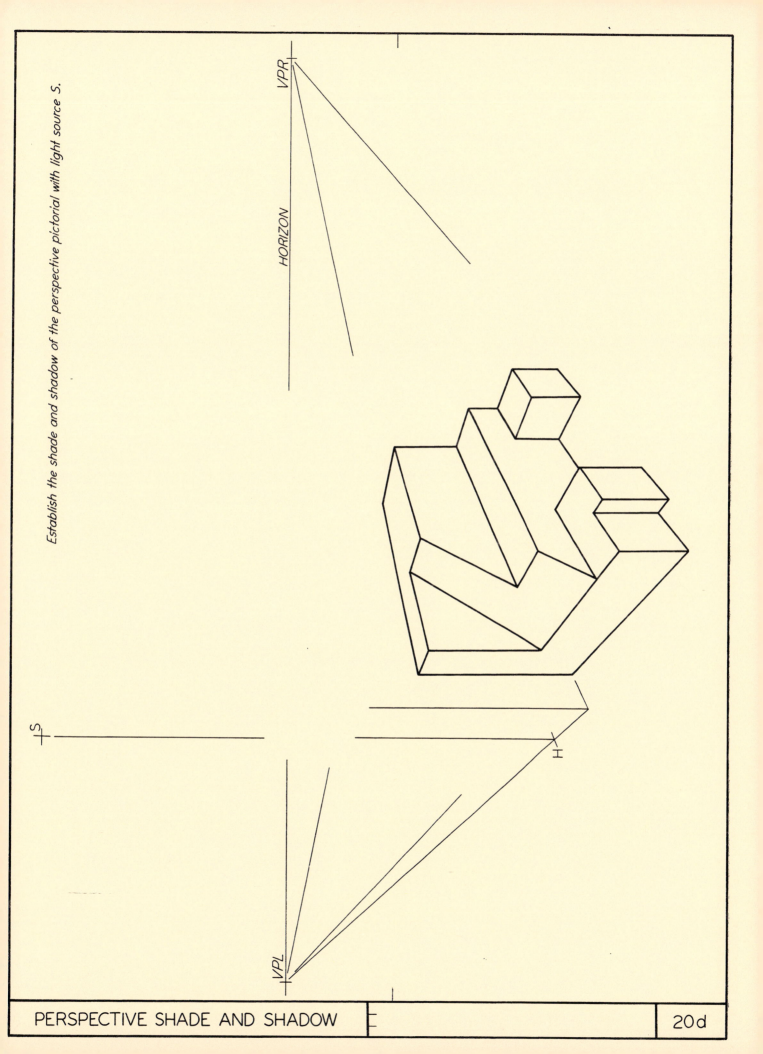

Establish the shade and shadow of the perspective pictorial with light source S.

VPR

HORIZON

VPL

H

S

1. Show the top view and the true-size view of the conic cut from the cone by plane A-A. Locate the focus and directrix and name the curve.

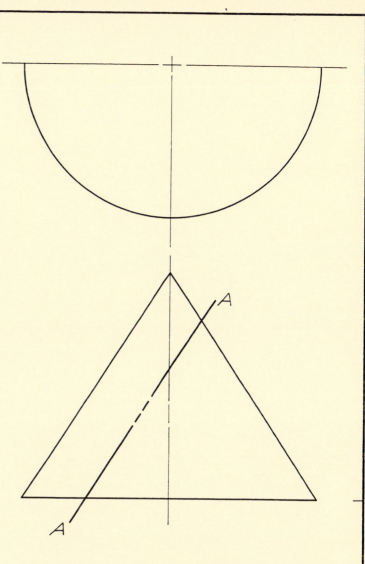

2. Show the true-size views of the bases of the truncated right circular cone. Name the curves.

1. Construct the polar gnomonic projection of the great circle course from Chicago (42°N, 88°W) to Moscow (56°N, 37°E). On this map show parallels at 10° intervals from 40°N to 80°N. Meridians are given at 10° intervals.

E
W
0° MERIDIAN

PLANE TANGENT AT N POLE

NORTH POLE

2. Plot the Mercator projection of the great circle course from Chicago to Moscow by determining in problem I the latitude of each intersection point of this course with a meridian and then locating the point on the Mercator map below.

Show the single constant bearing course from Chicago to Moscow on the Mercator map and then transfe this course to the gnomonic map of problem I.

ZERO MERIDIAN

40°
EQUATOR

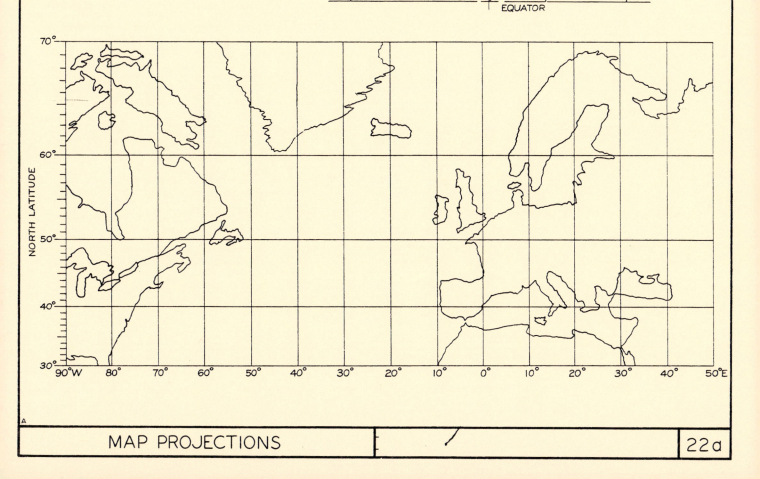

NORTH LATITUDE

70°

60°

50°

40°

30°

90°W 80° 70° 60° 50° 40° 30° 20° 10° 0° 10° 20° 30° 40° 50°E

MAP PROJECTIONS

22a

A

Locate the views of a spherical triangle ABC if side BC = 30°, side CA = 45°, and side BA = 65°.
Determine the angles at the vertices A, B, and C.

Angles –

A = ...

B = ...

C = ...

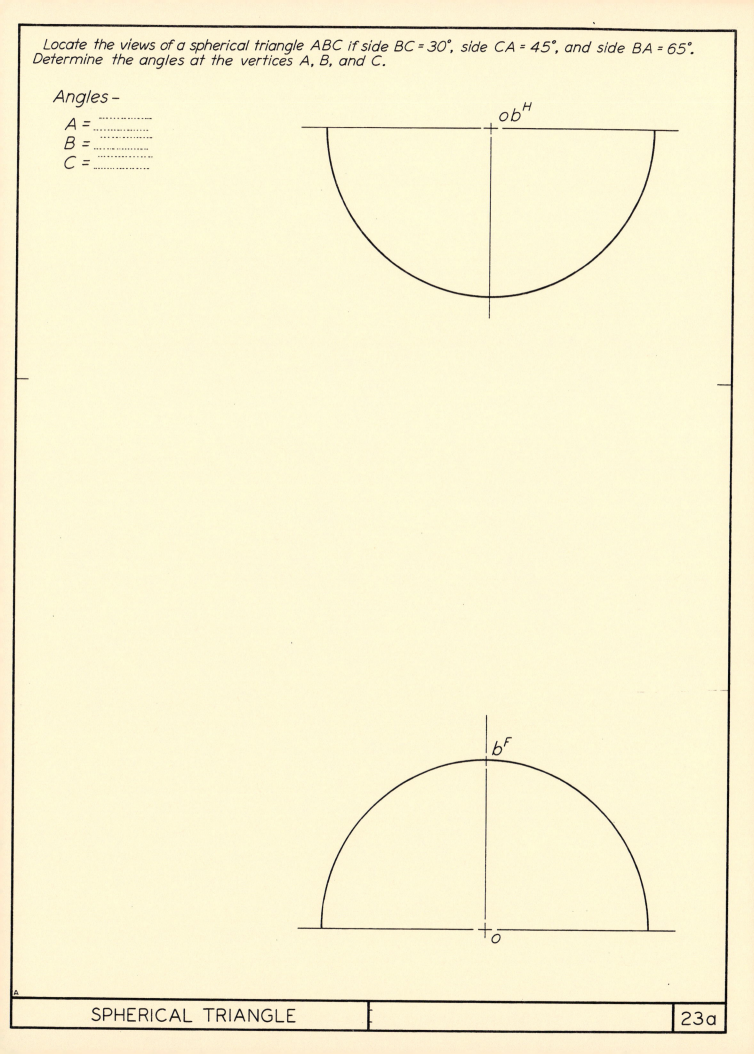

SPHERICAL TRIANGLE

23a

Obtain the great circle distance between point A, Lat. 50°N, Long. 150°W, and point C, Lat. 25°N, Long. 20°W.
Find the initial and final bearing of the great circle course from A to C.

DISTANCE - ....
INITIAL BEARING - ....
FINAL BEARING - ....

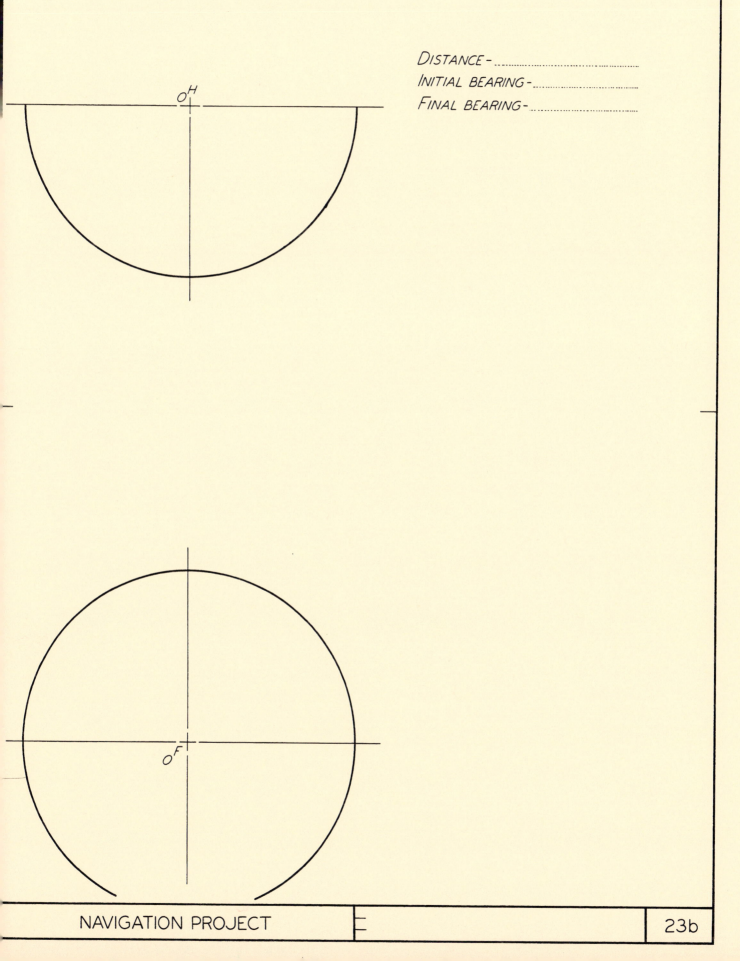

Determine the following:
 a. TL and views of the altitude of the pyramid.
 b. Dihedral angle formed by planes VCE and ABCE.
 c. Strike and dip of plane ABCE.
 d. Intersection of line MN and the pyramid.

VIEW 2 →

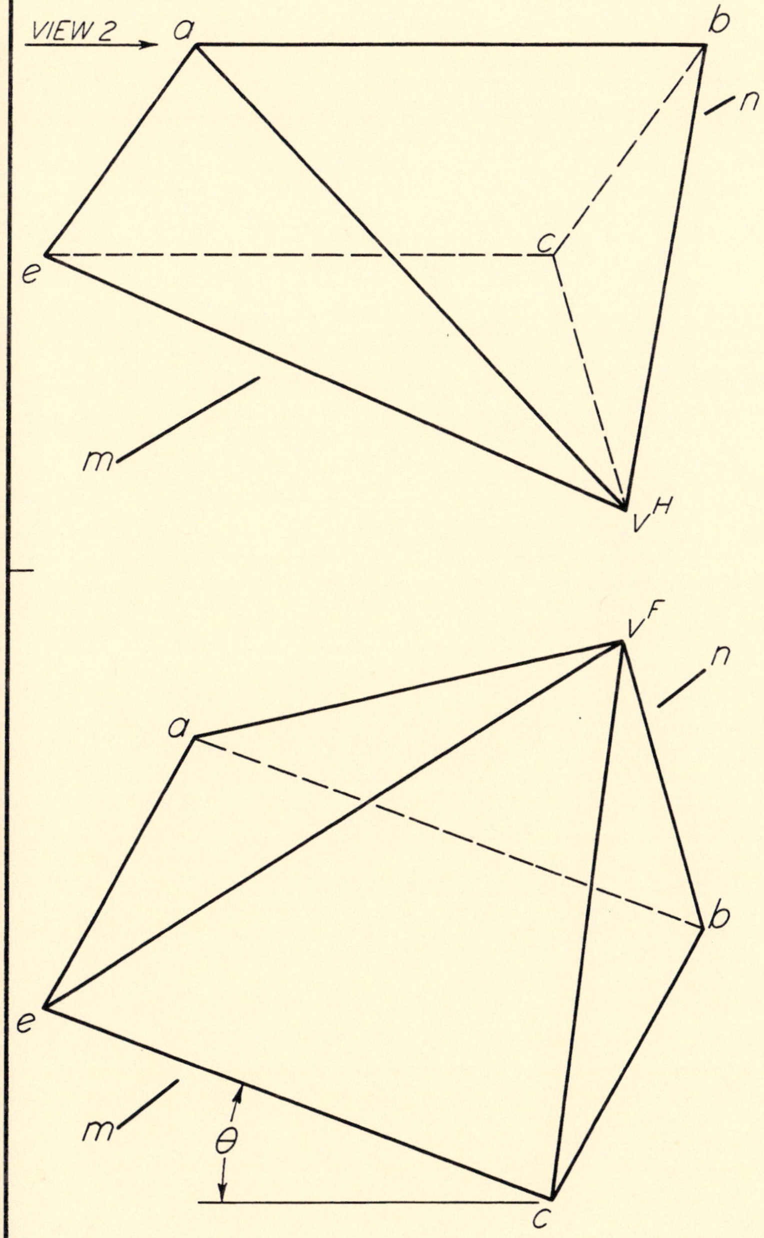

ALTITUDE- ....
DIHEDRAL ANGLE- ....
STRIKE- ....
DIP- ....

BASIC REVIEW PROJECTS

24d

Determine the following:
 a. The angle between the line CA and a profile plane.
 b. The views and true length of the altitude of the pyramid.
 c. The angle between the line VA and the plane ABC.
 d. The intersection of the limited plane MNO and the pyramid.

Check (√) the following for true or false:

	T	F
1. Plane ABC is true size in the top view.		
2. Line VC is perpendicular to the line VA.		
3. Angle θ is the true slope of the line CA.		
4. View 4 will show the dihedral angle between the planes VAC and VAB.		

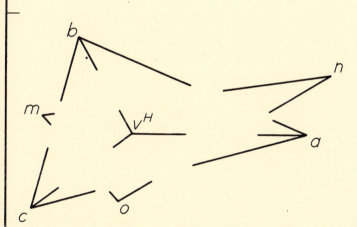

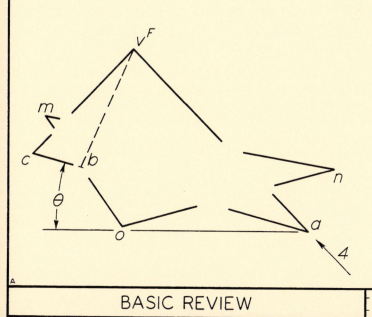

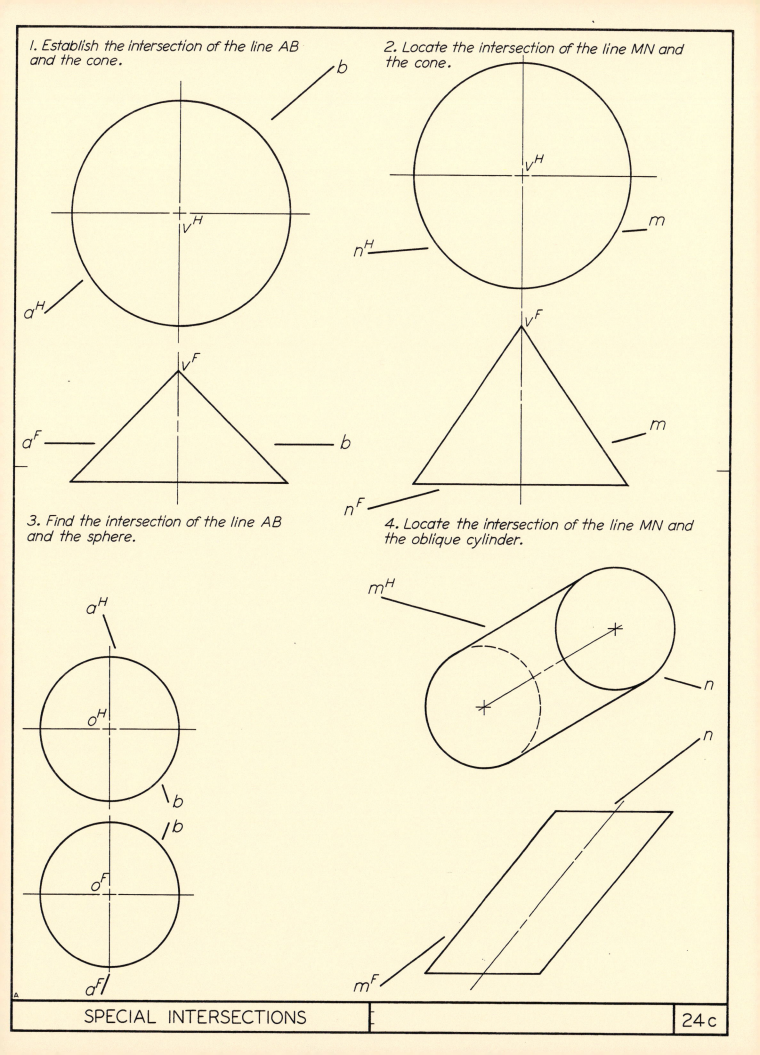

1. Establish the intersection of the line AB and the cone.

b

a^H

v^H

v^F

a^F _____ b

2. Locate the intersection of the line MN and the cone.

v^H

n^H

m

v^F

m

n^F

3. Find the intersection of the line AB and the sphere.

a^H

o^H

b

b

o^F

a^F

4. Locate the intersection of the line MN and the oblique cylinder.

m^H

n

n

m^F

SPECIAL INTERSECTIONS

24c

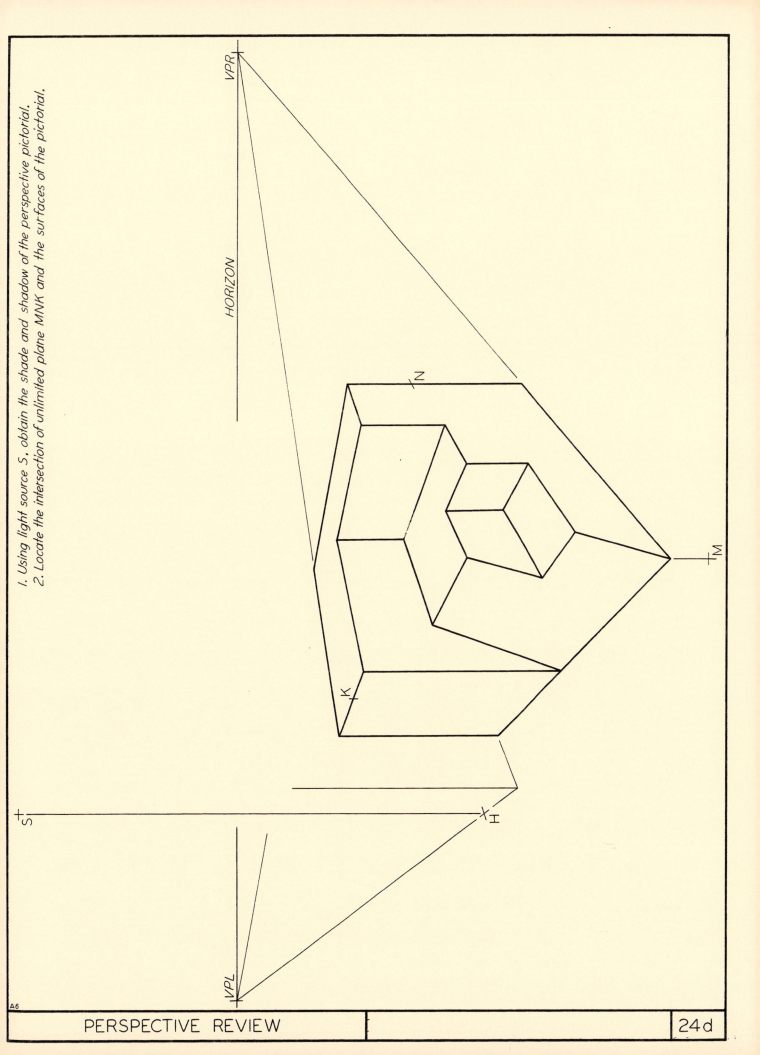

I. Using light source S, obtain the shade and shadow of the perspective pictorial.
2. Locate the intersection of unlimited plane MNK and the surfaces of the pictorial.

HORIZON

VPR

VPL

S

H

M

N

K

A6

PERSPECTIVE REVIEW

24d

1. Plot contour lines at 2 meter intervals.
2. On an overlay show contour lines and a nine-hole golf course, including clubhouse, parking, tennis courts, pool, etc.
3. Provide a three-dimensional model.

Scale: 1/4000.

71	64	55	47	40	37
71	58	47	43	41	37
66	56	43	49	43	41
60	50	47	54	48	47
70					
65	53	45	53	59	53	53
76	63	59	57	61	53	51
79	75	65	59	53	49	47
81	73	69	61	55	57	55
83	82	75	66	51	55	48

ROADWAY

GOLF COURSE LAYOUT

24e

1. Show contour lines at 5 meter intervals.
2. On an overlay, show contour lines and three hiking trails with grades not to exceed 10%.

Scale: 1/5000.

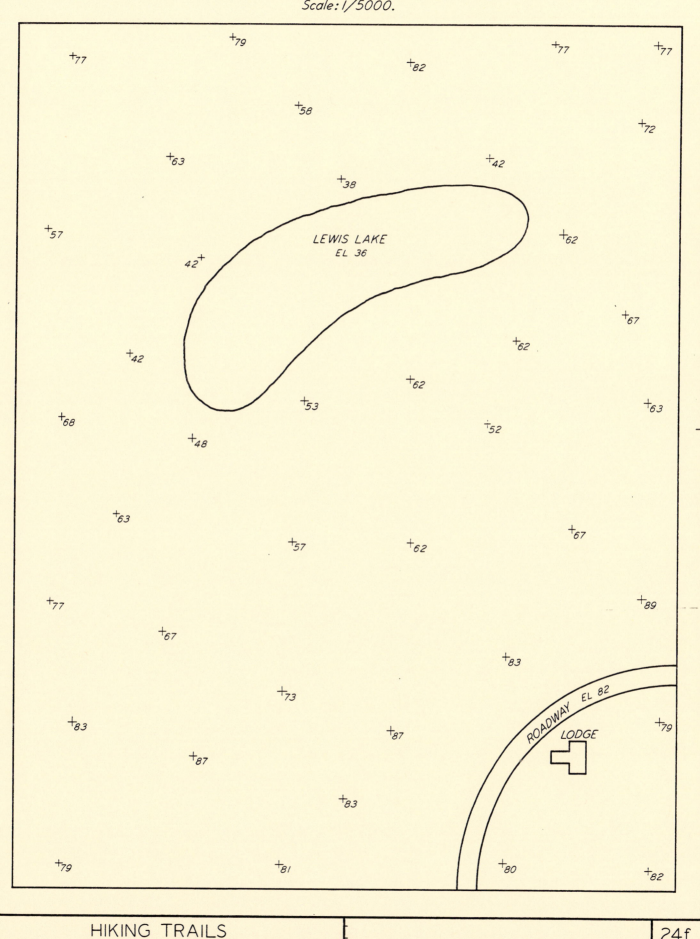

+79
+77
+82
+77 +77
+58
+72
+63
+42
+38
LEWIS LAKE
EL 36
+57
+62
42+
+67
+42
+62
+62
+53
+63
+48
+52
+63
+67
+57
+62
+77
+89
+67
+83
+73
ROADWAY EL 82
+83
+87 LODGE +79
+87
+83
+79
+81
+80
+82

A6

HIKING TRAILS   24f

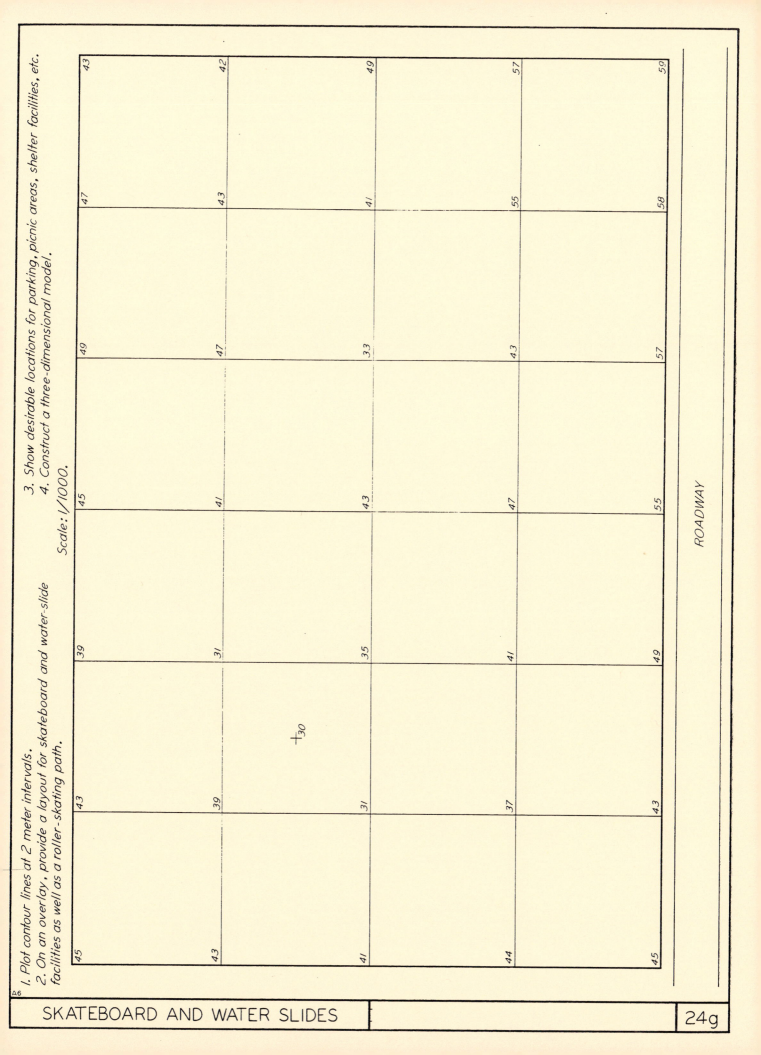

A6

1. Plot contour lines at 2 meter intervals.
2. On an overlay, provide a layout for skateboard and water-slide facilities as well as a roller-skating path.
3. Show desirable locations for parking, picnic areas, shelter facilities, etc.
4. Construct a three-dimensional model.

Scale: 1/1000.

ROADWAY

43	42	49	57	59
47	43	41	55	58
49	47	33	43	57
45	41	43	47	55
39	31	35	41	49
43	39	31	37	43
45	43	41	44	45

+30

SKATEBOARD AND WATER SLIDES

24g

1. Obtain the strike and dip of the plane ABC.
2. Find the distance between the surface of the sphere and plane ABC.
3. If point S is on the upper surface of the sphere, locate the views of the
orthographic projection of point S on plane ABC.

STRIKE - ....

DIP - ....

DISTANCE - ....

a

b^H

$\times s^H$

o^H

o^F

c

a

b^F

c

SPHERE PROJECT

24h

An aircraft at A is flying N-45° and diving at a rate of 2000 m   per minute. The indicated air speed is 180 knots. A ship at S is proceeding N-300° at 42 knots. How close will the two pass? Show their locations at the moment of closest approach. Distance scale 1:100 000
Velocity scale 1mm=100m/min

+S ^{H}

a^H+

a^F+

SEA LEVEL ——————————— +S ^{F} ——————

CALCULATIONS:

NON-COPLANAR VECTORS

B

24 i

THIS COMPUTER PROGRAM PROVIDES THE BEARING, TRUE LENGTH, AND GRADE OF LINE AB. THE BEARING IS EQUIVALENT TO THE TANGENT OF TRIANGLE INVOLVING LEGS X AND Z. THAT IS:

BEARING ANGLE = ATAN$\left(\frac{X}{Z}\right)$. THE TRUE LENGTH OF AB IS THE HYPOTENUSE OF THE RIGHT TRIANGLE WITH LEGS IDENTIFIED AS RISE AND RUN. OBSERVE THAT THE RUN = $\sqrt{X^2 + Z^2}$ AND RISE IS THE VERTICAL HEIGHT FROM B TO A. THE GRADE OF AB ALSO ENTAILS THE SAME RUN AND RISE. THAT IS:

GRADE = $\frac{RISE}{RUN}$ (100). NOTE THAT THE TOP VIEW LOCATION OF B IS A VARIABLE TO PERMIT A VARIETY OF SOLUTIONS. THE PROGRAM IS DESIGNED TO DRAW THE RISE, RUN TRIANGLE AND TO IDENTIFY THE SEVERAL ANSWERS.

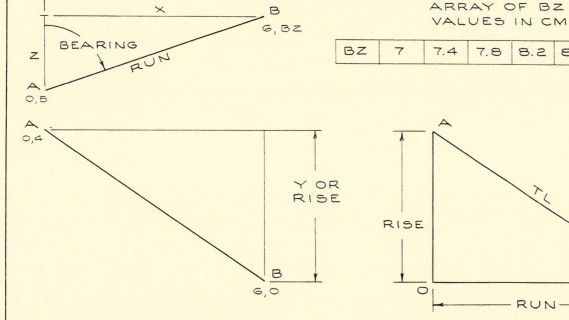

| BZ | 7 | 7.4 | 7.8 | 8.2 | 8.6 | 9 | 10 |

ARRAY OF BZ VALUES IN CM

COMMENTS

ACTIVATE COMPUTER, TYPE LOGIN

USER-ID, TYPE ME 102

PASSWORD, TYPE ME 102

AFTER OK, APPEARS, TYPE LD

TYPE PROJECT NAME, BTLLIN.

CHARACTER *80 IS USED TO STORE DATA ON 10 PROGRAM SPACES.

STORE ONE-LETTER RESPONSE.

STORE WHOLE-NUMBER VALUES.

FLOATING-POINT MODE VALUES.

BRIEF EXPLANATION OF THIS COMPUTER PROGRAM.

REFERENCE LINE.

USER ENTERS SELECTED BZ VALUE. FOR EXAMPLE: TYPE 7.

BEARING = ATAN$\left(\frac{X}{Z}\right)$ × 57.1 IN DEGREES.

RUN = $\sqrt{X^2 + Z^2}$

TLAB = $\sqrt{RISE^2 + RUN^2}$

COMPUTER INPUT

```
LOGIN
USER ID
PASSWORD
OK,
BTLLIN
CHARACTER *80 OUT(10)

CHARACTER *1 ANS
INTEGER *2 ID, I
REAL *4 BZ, RISE, RUN, BEARING,
& TLAB, GRADE
ID = O
PRINT *,'PROGRAM BTLLIN'
PRINT *,'USER PROVIDES BZ'
PRINT *,'PROGRAM DISPLAYS'
PRINT *,'1) BEARING OF LINE'
PRINT *,'2) TRUE LENGTH OF LINE'
PRINT *,'3) GRADE OF LINE'
PRINT *,'4) PLOT OF THE TL'
100 CONTINUE
PRINT *,'ENTER BZ'
READ (1 *, ERROR =100) BZ
BEAR = ATAN (6./(BZ - 5.)) *57.1
RUN = SQRT (4. **2+(BZ-5.) **2)
TLAB = SQRT (4. **2+RUN **2)
```

COMPUTER GRAPHICS (TRUE LENGTH)   25 a

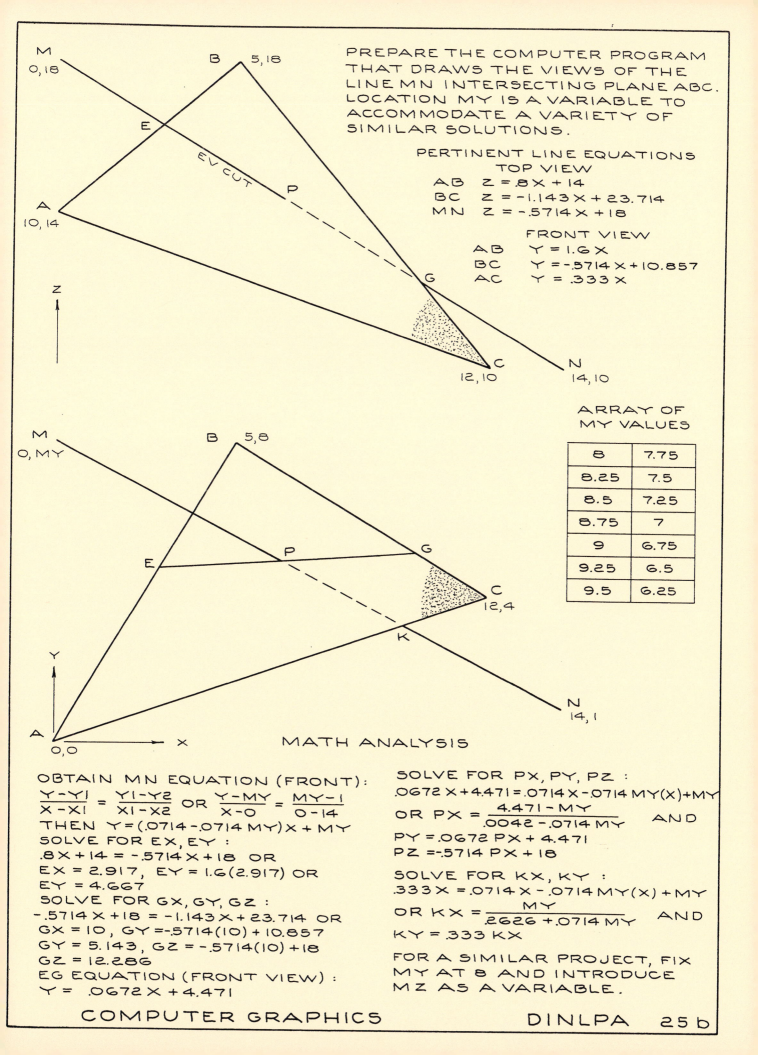

PREPARE THE COMPUTER PROGRAM THAT DRAWS THE VIEWS OF THE LINE MN INTERSECTING PLANE ABC. LOCATION MY IS A VARIABLE TO ACCOMMODATE A VARIETY OF SIMILAR SOLUTIONS.

PERTINENT LINE EQUATIONS
TOP VIEW

AB $Z = .8X + 14$
BC $Z = -1.143X + 23.714$
MN $Z = -.5714X + 18$

FRONT VIEW

AB $Y = 1.6X$
BC $Y = -.5714X + 10.857$
AC $Y = .333X$

M 0,18
B 5,18
E
EV CUT
P
A 10,14
Z
G
C 12,10
N 14,10

ARRAY OF MY VALUES

8	7.75
8.25	7.5
8.5	7.25
8.75	7
9	6.75
9.25	6.5
9.5	6.25

M 0,MY
B 5,8
E
P
G
C 12,4
K
A 0,0
Y
N 14,1
X

MATH ANALYSIS

OBTAIN MN EQUATION (FRONT):
$$\frac{Y-Y_1}{X-X_1} = \frac{Y_1-Y_2}{X_1-X_2} \quad OR \quad \frac{Y-MY}{X-0} = \frac{MY-1}{0-14}$$
THEN $Y = (.0714 - .0714\,MY)X + MY$
SOLVE FOR EX, EY :
$.8X + 14 = -.5714X + 18$ OR
$EX = 2.917$, $EY = 1.6(2.917)$ OR
$EY = 4.667$
SOLVE FOR GX, GY, GZ :
$-.5714X + 18 = -1.143X + 23.714$ OR
$GX = 10$, $GY = -.5714(10) + 10.857$
$GY = 5.143$, $GZ = -.5714(10) + 18$
$GZ = 12.286$
EG EQUATION (FRONT VIEW) :
$Y = .0672X + 4.471$

SOLVE FOR PX, PY, PZ :
$.0672X + 4.471 = .0714X - .0714\,MY(X) + MY$
OR $PX = \dfrac{4.471 - MY}{.0042 - .0714\,MY}$ AND
$PY = .0672\,PX + 4.471$
$PZ = -.5714\,PX + 18$

SOLVE FOR KX, KY :
$.333X = .0714X - .0714\,MY(X) + MY$
OR $KX = \dfrac{MY}{.2626 + .0714\,MY}$ AND
$KY = .333\,KX$

FOR A SIMILAR PROJECT, FIX MY AT 8 AND INTRODUCE MZ AS A VARIABLE.

COMPUTER GRAPHICS   DINLPA   25 b

1. STUDY THE ANALYSIS AND MATH THAT PROVIDE THE INTERSECTION OF THE TWO PLANES. PREPARE A COMPUTER PROGRAM TO DRAW THE VIEWS.

LINE EQUATIONS AND MATH
TOP VIEW   AB $Z = 1.5X + 7$
BC $Z = -.75X + 11.5$, AC $Z = 7$
MN $Z = X + 6$, MK $Z = 6$
LINE NK $Z = -X + 14$
FRONT VIEW AB $Y = 2.5X$
BC $Y = -X + 7$, AC $Y = .167X$
MK $Y = 4$, MN $Y = -X + 4$
LINE NK $Y = X - 4$
SOLVE FOR LOCATION G :
$2.5X = -X + 4$ OR $GX = 1.143$
$GY = 2.5(1.143)$ OR $GY = 2.858$
$GZ = 1.5(1.143) + 7$, $GZ = 8.715$
SOLVE FOR LOCATION J :
$.167X = -X + 4$ OR $JX = 3.428$
$JY = -3.428 + 4$, $JY = .572$
AND $JZ = 7$
GJ EQUATION TOP VIEW :
$Z = -.75X + 9.571$
SOLVE FOR LOCATION E :
WHERE $EY = 4$, $4 = -EX + 7$ OR
$EX = 3$ AND $EZ = 6$
SOLVE FOR LOCATION S :
$X - 4 = -X + 7$ OR $SX = 5.5$
$SY = 5.5 - 4$ OR $SY = 1.5$
$SZ = -5.5 + 14$ OR $SZ = 8.5$
ES EQUATION TOP VIEW :
$Z = X + 3$;   OBTAIN PX, PZ, PY :
$X + 6 = -.75X + 9.571$ OR $PX = 2.041$
$PZ = 2.041 + 6$ OR $PZ = 8.041$
$PY = -2.041 + 4$ OR $PY = 1.959$
ALSO $QX = 4.857$, $QZ = 7.857$ AND
$QY = 2.143$; $UZ = 7$, $UX = 1$
$VX = 3.143$, $VZ = 9.143$
$DY = 4$, $DX = 1.6$; $OX = 4.8$, $OY = .8$

2. SOLVE GRAPHICALLY FOR THE INTERSECTION OF THE PLANES. IF ASSIGNED, PREPARE THE MATH AND COMPUTER PROGRAM TO DRAW THE VIEWS.

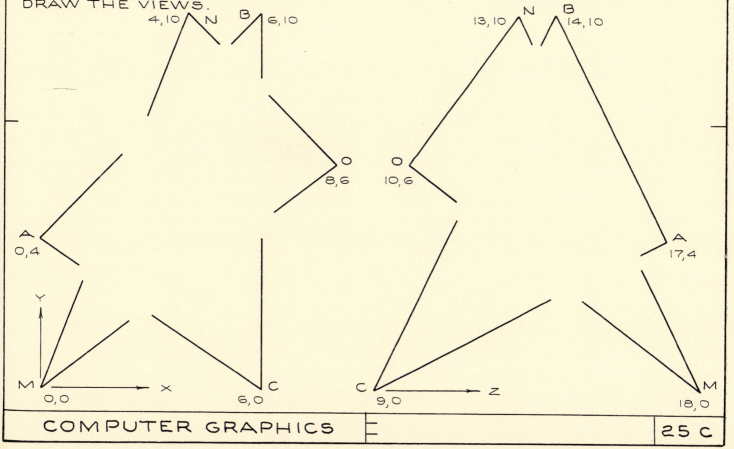

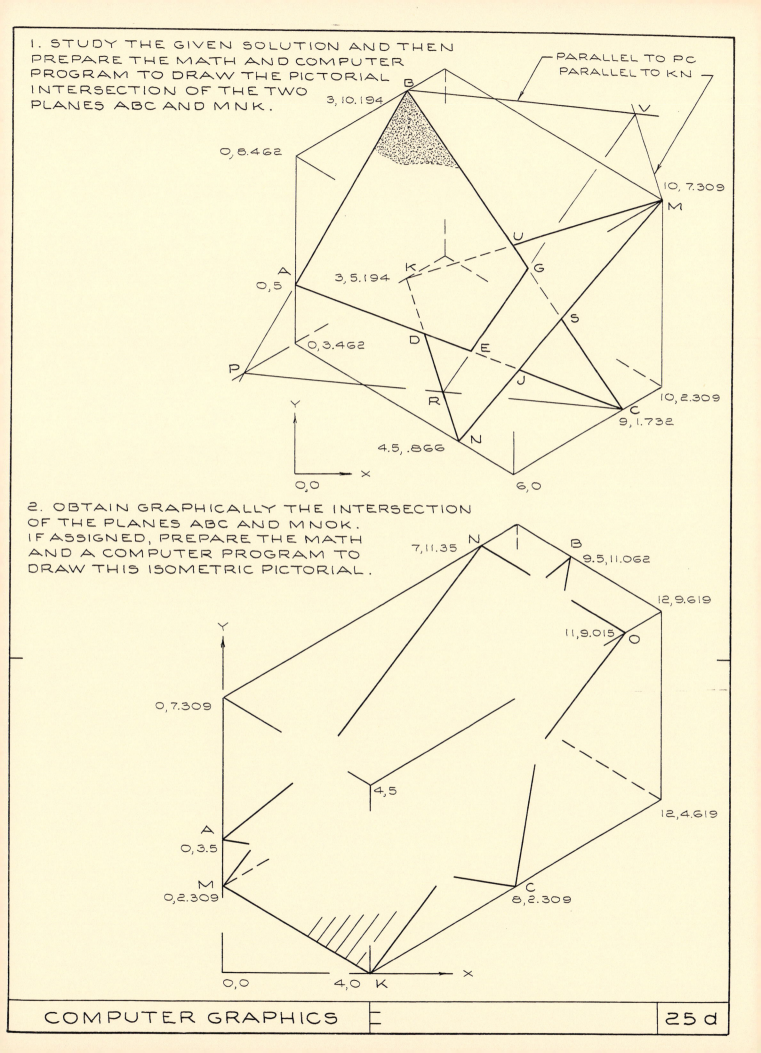

1. STUDY THE GIVEN SOLUTION AND THEN PREPARE THE MATH AND COMPUTER PROGRAM TO DRAW THE PICTORIAL INTERSECTION OF THE TWO PLANES ABC AND MNK.

PARALLEL TO PC
PARALLEL TO KN

B 3, 10.194

0, 8.462

V

10, 7.309 M

U

K 3, 5.194

G

A 0, 5

S

0, 3.462 D E

P

J

10, 2.309

R

C 9, 1.732

Y

N 4.5, .866

X

0, 0

6, 0

2. OBTAIN GRAPHICALLY THE INTERSECTION OF THE PLANES ABC AND MNOK. IF ASSIGNED, PREPARE THE MATH AND A COMPUTER PROGRAM TO DRAW THIS ISOMETRIC PICTORIAL.

N 7, 11.35

B 9.5, 11.062

12, 9.619

11, 9.015 O

Y

0, 7.309

4, 5

12, 4.619

A 0, 3.5

M 0, 2.309

C 8, 2.309

X

0, 0

4, 0 K

COMPUTER GRAPHICS

25d

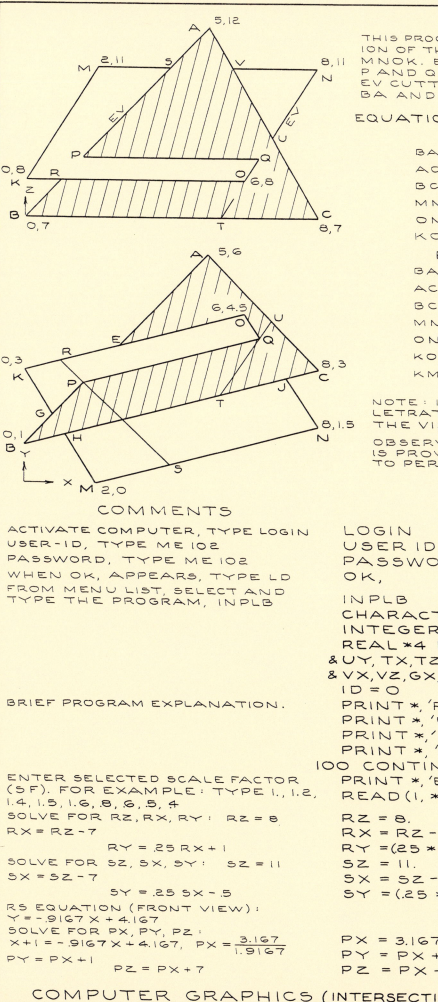

THIS PROGRAM PROVIDES THE INTERSECT-
ION OF THE TWO PLANES ABC AND
MNOK. ESSENTIAL PIERCING POINTS
P AND Q ARE ESTABLISHED USING
EV CUTTING PLANES THRU LINES
BA AND ON IN THE TOP VIEW.

EQUATIONS OF PERTINENT LINES
TOP VIEW

BA	$Z = X + 7$
AC	$Z = -1.667 X + 20.333$
BC	$Z = 7$
MN	$Z = 11$
ON	$Z = 1.5 X - 1$
KO	$Z = 8$

FRONT VIEW

BA	$Y = X + 1$
AC	$Y = -X + 11$
BC	$Y = .25 X + 1$
MN	$Y = .25 X - .5$
ON	$Y = -1.5 X + 13.5$
KO	$Y = .25 X + 3$
KM	$Y = -1.5 X + 3$

NOTE: INTRODUCE MECHANICAL OR
LETRATONE SHADING TO ENHANCE
THE VISIBILITY.

OBSERVE THAT A SCALE FACTOR
IS PROVIDED BY THE OPERATOR
TO PERMIT A VARIETY OF SIZES.

COMMENTS

ACTIVATE COMPUTER, TYPE LOGIN
USER-ID, TYPE ME 102
PASSWORD, TYPE ME 102
WHEN OK, APPEARS, TYPE LD
FROM MENU LIST, SELECT AND
TYPE THE PROGRAM, INPLB

BRIEF PROGRAM EXPLANATION.

ENTER SELECTED SCALE FACTOR
(SF). FOR EXAMPLE: TYPE 1., 1.2,
1.4, 1.5, 1.6, .8, .6, .5, .4
SOLVE FOR RZ, RX, RY: RZ = 8
RX = RZ - 7
$\qquad$ RY = .25 RX + 1
SOLVE FOR SZ, SX, SY: SZ = 11
SX = SZ - 7
$\qquad$ SY = .25 SX - .5
RS EQUATION (FRONT VIEW):
$Y = -.9167 X + 4.167$
SOLVE FOR PX, PY, PZ:
$X + 1 = -.9167 X + 4.167$, $PX = \dfrac{3.167}{1.9167}$
PY = PX + 1
$\qquad$ PZ = PX + 7

COMPUTER INPUT

```
LOGIN
USER ID
PASSWORD
OK,

INPLB
CHARACTER *1 ANS
INTEGER *2 ID, I
REAL *4 RX, RZ, RY, SX, SZ, SY, UX, UZ,
&UY, TX, TZ, TY, PX, PY, PZ, QX, QY, QZ,
&VX, VZ, GX, GY, EX, EY, HX, HY, JX, JY
ID = 0
PRINT *, 'PROGRAM INPLB'
PRINT *, 'USER PROVIDES SCALE'
PRINT *, 'THE PROGRAM DISPLAYS'
PRINT *, 'PLOT OF VIEWS'
100 CONTINUE
PRINT *, 'ENTER SCALE FACTOR'
READ (I, *, ERR = 100) SF

RZ = 8.
RX = RZ - 7.
RY = (25 * RX) + 1.
SZ = 11.
SX = SZ - 7.
SY = (.25 * SX) - .5



PX = 3.167/1.9167
PY = PX + 1.
PZ = PX + 7.
```

COMPUTER GRAPHICS (INTERSECTING PLANES)

REVIEW SHEET CGI FOR LOGIN AND TL OF LINE INFORMATION. THIS PROJECT ENTAILS THE HALF SHEET-METAL DEVELOPMENT OF A RECTANGULAR PYRAMID, PYRDEV. THE PYRAMID IS DIMENSIONED USING THE GENERAL VALUES FOR W, H, AND DP. FOR THE DEVELOPMENT, LENGTHS VA AND VB NEED TO BE SECURED AS WELL AS THE MORE CONVENIENT TL OF EDGES AB & BC. SEVERAL ANGLES AS WELL AS COORDINATES X, Y, XI, AND YI ARE ALSO NEEDED.

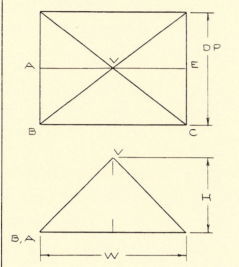

$$\text{TL OF } V\bar{A} = \sqrt{H^2 + \left(\frac{W}{2}\right)^2}$$

$$\text{RISE OF } VB = H \qquad \text{RUN} = \sqrt{\left(\frac{DP}{2}\right)^2 + \left(\frac{W}{2}\right)^2}$$

$$\text{TL OF } VB = \sqrt{\text{RISE}^2 + \text{RUN}^2}$$

$$\text{IN DEVEL} \quad \text{TAN ANGABV} = \frac{VA}{AB} \quad \text{OR} \quad \frac{VA(2)}{DP}$$

USING COSINE LAW FOR TRIANGLE VBC :

$$\cos(VBC) = \frac{BC^2 + VB^2 - VC^2}{2(BC)(VB)} \qquad \text{NOTE } VC = VB$$

ANGCBO = ANGABV + ANGVBC − 90°

$$\text{SINCE 1 RADIAN} = 57.3° \qquad 90° = \frac{90}{57.3} = 1.57 \text{ RAD}$$

THEN ANGCBO = ANGABV + ANGVBC − 1.57

USE SIN AND COS FUNCTIONS OF ANGCBO TO OBTAIN COORDINATES Y AND X RESPECTIVELY. ESTABLISH ANGSCE AND XI AND YI. NOTE ANGBCE = ANGVBC

SUGGESTED VALUES

H	W	DP
2	4	3
2.4	4.4	3.4
2.8	4.8	3.8
3.2	5.2	4.2
3.6	5.6	4.6
4	6	5
4.4	6.4	5.4

VALUES IN CM

HALF DEVELOPMENT

GENERAL COMMENTS

TYPE LOGIN
TYPE THE USER-ID, ME102
TYPE THE PASSWORD, ME102
AFTER OK, APPEAR ON THE TERMINAL, REQUEST LIST DIRECTORY, TYPE LD. SELECT AND TYPE PROJECT, PYRDEV VARIABLES OUT (1) THRU OUT (10) WILL BE USED TO STORE DATA OF UP TO 80 CHARACTERS EACH.
ANS *1 WILL BE USED TO STORE ONE-LETTER RESPONSES TO QUESTIONS; FOR EXAMPLE : Y FOR YES.
INTEGER *2 ID, I WILL BE EMPLOYED TO STORE WHOLE NUMBER VARIABLES. THESE VARIABLES ARE IN FLOATING POINT MODE TO ACCEPT DECIMAL VALUES. THIS ENTRY SETS LINE LOCATION AT O. ID IS USED TO INDICATE WHERE TO SHOW DATA OR ANS. FOR EXAMPLE : O FOR TERMINAL, 22 FOR PLOTTER. A SHORT PROGRAM EXPLANATION IS PROVIDED WITH PRINT STATEMENTS.

THE NO. 100 IS USED TO REFERENCE THAT LINE IN THE PROGRAM. THE CONTINUE STATEMENT PERMITS THE PROGRAM TO PROGRESS.
THE USER IS NEXT REQUESTED TO ENTER ASSIGNED VALUES OF H, W, AND DP. FOR EXAMPLE : TYPE 2., 4., 3. THIS LINE WILL IDENTIFY THESE VALUES AND STORE THEM IN THE RESPECTIVE VARIABLES. A SELECTION ERROR WILL RETURN THE PROGRAM TO LINE 100.

$$\text{TL OF } V\bar{A} = \sqrt{H^2 + \left(\frac{W}{2}\right)^2}$$

RISE OF VB = H

$$\text{RUN OF } VB = \sqrt{\left(\frac{DP}{2}\right)^2 + \left(\frac{W}{2}\right)^2}$$

$$\text{TL OF } VB = \sqrt{\text{RISE}^2 + \text{RUN}^2} \qquad AB = \frac{DP}{2}$$

NOTE THAT VC = VB & VE = VA.

$$\text{IN DEVELOPMENT} \quad \text{TAN ANGABV} = \frac{VA}{AB}$$

$$\text{OR ANGABV} = \text{TAN}^{-1} \frac{VA(2)}{DP} \qquad BC = W$$

USING COSINE LAW :

$$\cos \text{ANGVBC} = \frac{BC^2 + VB^2 - VC^2}{2(BC)(VB)}$$

COMPUTER INPUT

```
CHARACTER *80 OUT(10)

CHARACTER *1 ANS

INTEGER *2 ID, I

REAL *4 H, W, DP, X, Y, XI, YI, ANGABV,
& ANGBCO, ANGVCO, ANGOCE, ANGSCE
ID = O

PRINT *,'PROGRAM PYRDEV'
PRINT *,'USER PROVIDES SELECTED
VALUES OF H, W, AND DP'
PRINT *,'THE PROGRAM CALCULATES:'
PRINT *,  'DEVELOPMENT PLOT'

100 CONTINUE

PRINT *,'ENTER H, W, DP'


READ (1, *, ERR = 100) H, W, DP

VA = SQRT(H**2 + (W/2.)**2)
RISE = H
RUN = SQRT((DP/2.)**2 + (W/2.)**2)
VB = SQRT(RISE**2 + RUN**2)
AB = DP/2.
ANGABV = ATAN(VA/AB)
BC = W

ANGVBC = ACOS(BC/(2.*VB))
```

COMPUTER GRAPHICS (DEVELOPMENT)

FOR THE SHADOW OF THE ISOMETRIC PICTORIAL,
A CONVENIENT 45° ANGLE FOR LIGHT RAY AB HAS
BEEN SELECTED, FIG. I. AN INITIAL CALCULATION
IS NEEDED TO OBTAIN ANGLE (ANG). SINCE JUST
A SINGLE VALUE EXISTS FOR THIS ANGLE, A
HAND CALCULATOR HAS BEEN EMPLOYED.

IN TRIANGLE CFD, $\sin(CDF) = \dfrac{CF}{CD}$

OR $CF = \sin(30°)(CD)$, $CF = .5 \times 5 = 2.5$

$FD = \cos(30°)(CD)$, $FD = .866 \times 5 = 4.33$

IN 45° TRIANGLE AFE, $AF = AC + CF$, $= 5 + 2.5 = 7.5$
AND $FE = AF$ OR 7.5; $DE = FE - FD$, $= 7.5 - 4.33 = 3.17$

IN TRIANGLE BDE: $\dfrac{DB}{DE} = \dfrac{\sin(45°)}{\sin(105°)}$

THEN $DB = \dfrac{.707}{.966}(3.17) = 2.32$

IN TRIANGLE CBD, USING THIS LAW OF COSINES:

$a^2 = b^2 + c^2 - 2bc(\cos A)$ OR

$\overline{CB}^2 = \overline{CD}^2 + \overline{DB}^2 - 2(CD)(DB) \times \cos(CDB)$

$\overline{CB}^2 = 5^2 + 2.32^2 - 2(5)(2.32) \times (-.5)$

$\overline{CB}^2 = 41.98$ OR $CB = 6.48$

IN TRIANGLE ABC: $\dfrac{\sin A}{CB} = \dfrac{\sin B}{AC}$

OR $\sin B = \dfrac{\sin A \cdot (AC)}{CB} = \dfrac{.707(5)}{6.48} = .5455$

ANGLE $B = \sin^{-1}(.5455)$, ANGLE $B = 33°$

ANGLE $ACB = 180° - (33° + 45°) = 102°$

ANGLE $ANG = 102° - 90° = 12°$

FOR THE ISOMETRIC PICTORIAL, DIMENSIONS ARE SHOWN
IN GENERAL TERMS SO THAT MANY SOLUTIONS CAN BE
OBTAINED. FIRST THE PROGRAM IS ESTABLISHED TO
PRODUCE THE PICTORIAL. THEN CALCULATIONS ARE
INTRODUCED TO OUTLINE THE VISIBLE SHADOW AREA.
REFER TO FIGURE 2 BELOW.

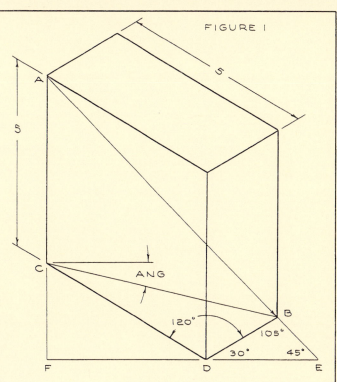

FIGURE I

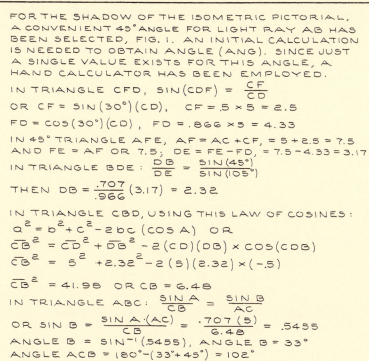

FIGURE 2

SUGGESTED VALUES

H	W	DP
2.5	4	2
3.2	4.4	2.2
3.8	4.8	2.4
4.2	5.2	2.6
4.6	5.6	2.8
5.0	6.0	3.0
5.4	6.4	3.2
5.8	6.8	3.4
6.2	7.2	3.6
6.6	7.6	3.8
7.0	8.0	4.0
7.4	8.4	4.2

VALUES IN CM

ABBREVIATED COMMENTS

TYPE LOGIN

USER-ID, TYPE ME102

PASSWORD, TYPE ME102

AFTER OK, SIGNAL APPEARS, TYPE
LD. ME102 MENU IS LISTED.
TYPE THE DESIRED PROGRAM:
ISOSHA

PRINT SHORT EXPLANATION OF
THE PROGRAM.

COMPUTER INPUT

```
LOGIN

USER ID

PASSWORD

OK,

ISOSHA

CHARACTER *1 ANS

INTEGER *2 ID, I

REAL *4 H, W, DP, X, Y, X1, Y1, X2, Y2, X3, Y3, Z0
ID = 0
PRINT *, 'PROGRAM ISOSHA'
PRINT *, 'USER PROVIDES H, W, DP'
PRINT *, 'PROG. FINDS X, Y, X1, Y1, X2, Y2, X3, Y3, Z0'
PRINT *, 'PLOT OF PICTORIAL AND SHADOW'
```

COMPUTER GRAPHICS

25 g

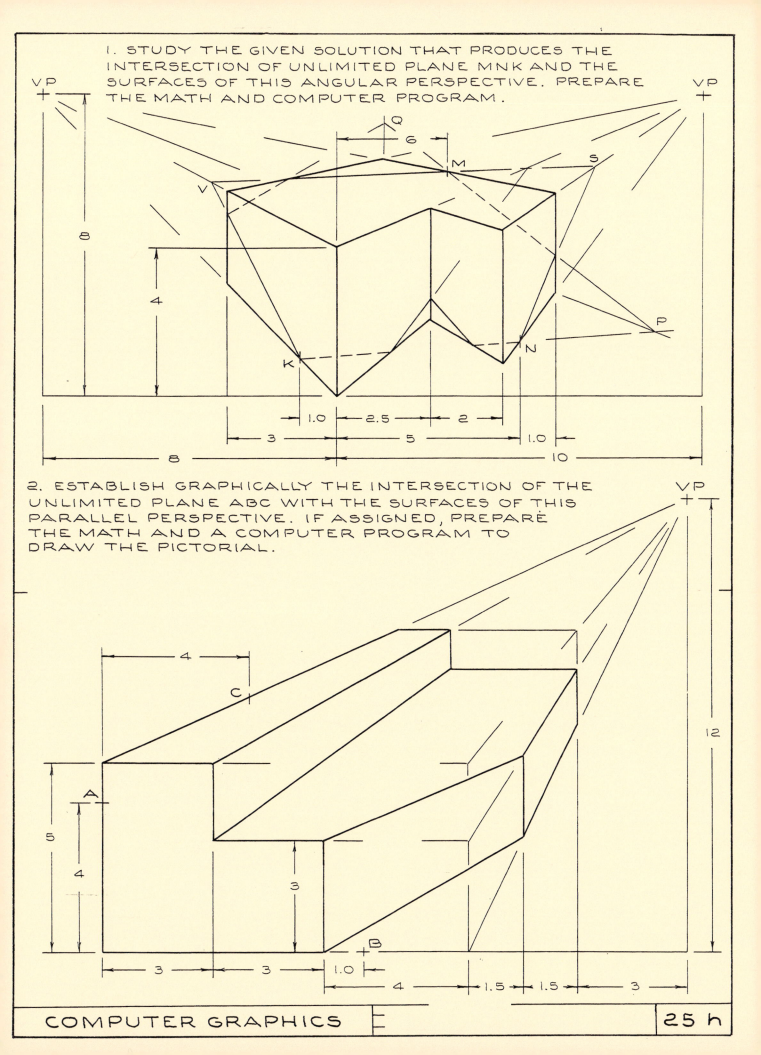

1. STUDY THE GIVEN SOLUTION THAT PRODUCES THE
INTERSECTION OF UNLIMITED PLANE MNK AND THE
SURFACES OF THIS ANGULAR PERSPECTIVE. PREPARE
THE MATH AND COMPUTER PROGRAM.

VP

VP

2. ESTABLISH GRAPHICALLY THE INTERSECTION OF THE
UNLIMITED PLANE ABC WITH THE SURFACES OF THIS
PARALLEL PERSPECTIVE. IF ASSIGNED, PREPARE
THE MATH AND A COMPUTER PROGRAM TO
DRAW THE PICTORIAL.

VP

COMPUTER GRAPHICS   25 h